THE REJECTION OF CONSEQUENTIALISM

THE REJECTION OF CONSEQUENTIALISM

*A Philosophical Investigation
of the Considerations Underlying
Rival Moral Conceptions*

by
SAMUEL SCHEFFLER

CLARENDON PRESS · OXFORD

Oxford University Press, Walton Street, Oxford OX2 6DP

London New York Toronto
Delhi Bombay Calcutta Madras Karachi
Kuala Lumpur Singapore Hong Kong Tokyo
Nairobi Dar es Salaam Cape Town
Melbourne Auckland

and associated companies in
Beirut Berlin Ibadan Mexico City Nicosia

Published in the United States by
Oxford University Press, New York

British Library Cataloguing in Publication Data

Scheffler, Samuel
    The rejection of consequentialism.
    1. Ethics
    I. Title
    170   BJ1012
    ISBN 0-19-824657-9
    ISBN 0-19-824741-9 Pbk.

Library of Congress Cataloguing in Publication Data

Scheffler, Samuel, 1951–
    The rejection of consequentialism.
    Includes index.
    1. Consequentialism (Ethics)   I. Title.
    BJ1031.S33   171'.5   81-18867
    ISBN 0-19-824657-9 AACR2
    ISBN 0-19-824741-9 Pbk.

Printed in Great Britain by
Hazell Watson & Viney Limited
Aylesbury, Bucks

For
Israel Scheffler
and
Rosalind Z. Scheffler

PREFACE

ACCORDING to an ancient if occasionally unfashionable view, the subject matter of moral philosophy is organized in the first instance around the question of how people ought to live their lives. That is certainly how I conceive of the subject, and as a consequence it has sometimes seemed to me that only a fool or a fanatic could seriously think himself 'professionally' competent to express and defend views in this area. Despite these scruples, which perhaps represent my better judgement, I am submitting the work that follows for the reader's consideration. In mitigation, I can only say that if the subject matter of moral philosophy is vast and daunting, as it is, and if the complexity and power of the experiences that typically prompt moral reflection sometimes make the theorist's abstractions seem hollow and glib, as they do, it is also true that the question which animates the subject as I conceive it is vivid and gripping and demands our attention, even if all too often we acknowledge the demand only by contriving to ignore it.

This book grows out of a dissertation which I submitted for the Ph.D. at Princeton in 1977. But my interest in the topics it deals with is as longstanding as my interest in philosophy itself. The first philosophy course I took as an undergraduate at Harvard was a course on ethics taught by Roderick Firth. At the time, I found myself strongly drawn to the deontological views, though not the epistemological intuitionism, of W. D. Ross, and utilitarianism I found thoroughly abhorrent. Rejecting Ross's own intuitionism, I began to worry about how a deontological view might be defended. My worries have only increased since that time, as the reader of this book will discover, and have led me in directions that have sometimes surprised and dismayed me. This book charts the current state of my thinking.

My debts are many and large, and I will mention only the greatest of them. A memorable seminar taught by Thomas Nagel during my first year as a graduate student at Princeton convinced me that I wanted to undertake the project which eventually became my dissertation. As a teacher and as a dissertation adviser, Nagel was everything a student could hope for, and more. My debt to him is greater than any brief acknowledgement could begin to suggest.

In the course of writing my dissertation, I was greatly helped by long and frequent discussions with John Campbell, Peter Railton, and T. M. Scanlon. I am particularly indebted to Railton for helping me to appreciate for the first time the real force and power of a consequentialist view.

After the dissertation was completed, Railton and Gilbert Harman made fundamental criticisms which caused me to rethink the entire project.

When I began to write again two years later in Berkeley, I benefited greatly from the opportunity to discuss my work in seminars, and I am grateful to the students and colleagues who attended those seminars. More generally, I would like to thank the members of the Berkeley philosophy department for providing such a congenial and supportive environment in which to work. I am particularly grateful to Janet Broughton, Thompson Clarke, Linda Foy, and Barry Stroud.

I received extremely helpful written comments on the penultimate draft of my manuscript from Campbell and Railton, and also from Shelly Kagan. I am sure that they will not be fully satisfied with my attempts to meet their objections, but I am equally sure that the book has been much improved as a result of my attempts to respond to the points they raised. I am grateful to them for taking my views seriously, and for taking the time to express their reservations and make suggestions for improvement.

My debt to Derek Parfit is, quite simply, extraordinary. His written comments on several drafts were extremely helpful and led to major improvements at points far too numerous to acknowledge individually. Indeed, his written comments on the penultimate draft were almost as long as that draft itself, and I blush to think of the errors the book would have contained but for his detailed and sensitive criticism. For all of this, and also for his support and encouragement, I am very deeply grateful. In fact, I suspect that only those who have received comparable assistance from him, and they are by no means few in number, will be able to fully appreciate the real extent of my debt.

Since this work does grow out of my Ph.D. dissertation, I would like to take this opportunity to thank the Danforth Foundation for giving me fellowship support when I was a graduate student. Most of the final version of the book was completed during a period of leave which was extended beyond the normal length of time by a Humanities Research Fellowship from the University of California, Berkeley, and I would like to thank the University for making possible that period of free time.

Finally, I want to express my appreciation to Kathryn G. Dreith, who prepared the book's index, and whose assistance at the proofreading stage was invaluable.

SAMUEL SCHEFFLER
Berkeley, California
December, 1981

CONTENTS

I

THE PROJECT AND ITS MOTIVATION

As John Rawls has written, 'The two main concepts of ethics are those of the right and the good . . . The structure of an ethical theory is . . . largely determined by how it defines and connects these two basic notions.'[1] Among ethical theories, those that I call 'act-consequentialist' may be characterized roughly as follows. Such theories first specify some principle for ranking overall states of affairs from best to worst from an impersonal point of view. In other words, the rankings generated by the designated principle are not agent-relative; they do not vary from person to person, depending on what one's particular situation is. For they do not embody judgements about which overall states of affairs are best for particular individuals, but rather judgements about which states of affairs are best, all things considered, from an impartial standpoint. After giving some principle for generating such rankings, act-consequentialists then require that each agent in all cases act in such a way as to produce the highest-ranked state of affairs that he is in a position to produce.[2] Different act-consequentialist

---

[1] *A Theory of Justice* (Harvard University Press, 1971), p. 24.

[2] Obviously, this formulation is oversimplified. Most such theories do not require the agent to act in such a way as to produce the best actual state of affairs that is available. Rather they require that the agent perform the available act that has the highest expected value, where the expected value of an act is a function of each of its various possible outcomes and of their probabilities of occurrence. I will, however, continue to use the oversimplified formulation because it highlights the features of consequentialism that are relevant to this discussion. For my purposes, nothing is lost by avoiding the more complicated and more accurate formulation.

It should also be emphasized that when I speak of the act-consequentialist as requiring agents to produce the best overall outcomes or states of affairs, I do not mean that the act-consequentialist divides what happens into the act and the outcome, and

theories incorporate different conceptions of the overall good: that is, different principles for ranking overall states of affairs from best to worst. But all such theories share the same conception of the right which requires each agent in all cases to produce the best available outcome overall.

Act-consequentialism is not the only kind of consequentialism; other variants include rule-consequentialism and motive-consequentialism. These views typically differ somewhat from act-consequentialism in what they require of agents,[3] though they share with act-consequentialism the feature of ranking overall states of affairs impersonally, and the general idea that the best states of affairs are *somehow* to be promoted. I will not be discussing these other variants of consequentialism in this book. Although I believe that my main lines of argument could be modified to cover them, the only kind of consequentialism that I will actually consider in the book is act-consequentialism. Since this is so, and since the term 'act-consequentialism' is cumbersome, I will, beginning with the next paragraph and throughout the rest of the book, use the terms 'consequentialism' and 'consequentialist' to mean 'act-consequentialism' and 'act-consequentialist', except where I explicitly state otherwise. This is purely an abbreviatory device, adopted for the sake of simplicity and ease of exposition; it is not intended to suggest either that my discussion encompasses all of the various forms of consequentialism, or that act-consequentialism is the only legitimate form of consequentialism.

In contrast to consequentialist conceptions, standard deontological views maintain that it is sometimes wrong to do what will produce the best available outcome overall. In other words, these views incorporate what I shall call 'agent-centred restrictions': restrictions on action which have the effect of denying that there is any non-agent-relative principle for ranking overall states of affairs from best to worst such that it is

---

evaluates only the latter with his overall ranking principle. Rather, the act itself is initially evaluated as part of the overall outcome or state of affairs. The act-consequentialist first ranks overall outcomes, which are understood, in this broad way, to include the acts necessary to produce them, and then directs the agent to produce the best available outcome so construed.

[3] For some complications, see David Lyons, *Forms and Limits of Utilitarianism* (Oxford University Press, 1965).

always permissible to produce the best available state of affairs so characterized.

Classical utilitarianism, which ranks states of affairs according to the amount of total satisfaction they contain, is the most familiar consequentialist view.[4] But classical utilitarianism is widely thought to be too crude a theory. Although its defenders point with approval to its simplicity, critics charge that this simplicity is achieved at too high a cost. They argue that utilitarianism relies on implausible assumptions about human motivation, incorporates a strained and superficial view of the human good, and ignores a host of important considerations about justice, fairness, and the character of human agency. More generally, they accuse utilitarianism of relentless insensitivity to the nature of a person, and suggest that it has forfeited any serious claim to account for the complex and varied considerations that intrude on the moral life, and which give rise to the severest tests of our decency. Indeed, utilitarianism has gained a reputation for moral clumsiness that is unparalleled among ethical theories. Bernard Williams, writing that 'the simple-mindedness of utilitarianism disqualifies it totally', suggests that '[t]he day cannot be too far off in which we hear no more of it'.[5]

And yet that day refuses to come; we continue to hear a great

---

[4] To avoid confusion, there are a number of points about this characterization of the view that I call 'classical utilitarianism' which should be noted at the outset. First, I intend it to be understood that whenever I speak of this view as ranking states of affairs according to the amount of total or aggregate satisfaction they contain, I mean, of course, total *net* satisfaction (that is, total satisfaction minus dissatisfaction). Second, classical utilitarianism as I understand it is a view that has hedonistic and non-hedonistic variants. Thus in characterizing the view I have deliberately used the term 'satisfaction', which can be understood either hedonistically, as referring to a kind of feeling, or non-hedonistically, as referring to the satisfaction of people's preferences, whatever the preferences may be for. In the course of this book, I will distinguish between the hedonistic and non-hedonistic variants of classical utilitarianism only when the distinction is relevant to the topic under discussion. Whenever I do not make the distinction explicitly, the reader is to understand what I say as applying to both the hedonistic and non-hedonistic variants. Finally, the term 'utilitarianism' is used in the philosophical literature in connection with a wide range of moral views, from rule-utilitarianism to the principle that the right act maximizes average utility to the so-called 'ideal utilitarianism' associated with G. E. Moore. But I will use the term exclusively to refer to the classical act-utilitarianism described in the text.

[5] J. J. C. Smart and Bernard Williams, *Utilitarianism For and Against* (Cambridge University Press, 1973), p. 150.

deal about utilitarianism. Cynics may suppose that the explanation for this lies in the philosopher's penchant for keeping half-dead horses just barely alive so that he can continue to beat them with a moderately clear conscience. My diagnosis is different: I believe that utilitarianism refuses to fade from the scene in large part because, as the most familiar consequentialist theory, it is the major recognized normative theory incorporating the deeply plausible-sounding feature that one may always do what would lead to the best available outcome overall. Despite all of utilitarianism's faults (including, no doubt, its misidentification of the best outcomes), its incorporation of this one plausible feature is in my opinion responsible for its persistence. Moral conceptions that include agent-centred restrictions, of course, reject this feature. Although a full characterization and discussion of these restrictions will not be presented until Chapter Four, they have already been identified as restrictions on action which have the effect of denying that there is *any* non-agent-relative principle for ranking overall states of affairs such that it is always permissible to produce the best available state of affairs so construed. If an adequate theoretical rationale for such restrictions could be identified, it would provide a reason for rejecting utilitarianism's deeply plausible-sounding feature. But although, as I will indicate in Chapter Four, it is easy to think of cases in which agent-centred restrictions seem intuitively appropriate, and although such restrictions constitute the heart of most familiar deontological moral conceptions, it is, as I will also indicate in Chapter Four, surprisingly difficult to find persuasive hypotheses in the literature as to what their underlying theoretical rationale might be.

Faced with what I take to be serious difficulties in the attempt to provide an adequate rationale for agent-centred restrictions, and faced with the plausibility of the idea that it is always permissible to do what would have the best outcome overall, I wish in this book to reconsider the rejection of consequentialism. What I will do, more specifically, is to undertake a comparative examination of two different kinds of non-consequentialist moral conceptions. The standard deontological theories I call 'fully agent-centred' conceptions constitute the more familiar of these two kinds. By virtue of including agent-centred restrictions, these conceptions deny that there is any non-agent-relative principle for ranking overall states of affairs from best to worst such that it is always permissible to produce the best available state of affairs so characterized. And in addition to including such restrictions, these conceptions also deny that one must do what would have the best outcome overall on all of those occasions when the restrictions do *not* forbid it. In other words, fully agent-centred conceptions maintain that, given any impersonal principle for ranking overall states of affairs from best to worst, there will be some circumstances in which one is not permitted to produce the best available state of affairs, and still other circumstances in which one is permitted but not required to do so.

Non-consequentialist conceptions of the second kind I will consider are much less familiar. Indeed, I am unaware of any previous discussion of them in the literature. These 'hybrid' conceptions, as I refer to them, depart from consequentialism through their incorporation of something I call an 'agent-centred prerogative', which has the effect of denying that one is always required to produce the best overall states of affairs, and which is thus in some form a feature of fully agent-centred conceptions as well.[6] At the same time, however, hybrid conceptions are akin to consequentialist conceptions in their rejection of agent-centred restrictions: that is, in their acceptance of the idea that it is always permissible to do what would produce the best overall state of affairs. In other words, hybrid conceptions are like fully agent-centred conceptions and unlike consequentialist conceptions in maintaining that one need not always do what would produce the best outcome; but they are like consequentialist conceptions and unlike fully agent-centred conceptions in accepting the plausible-sounding idea that one *may* always do what would produce the best outcome.

The agent-centred prerogative, as I will argue, is responsive

---

[6]That is, since fully agent-centred conceptions do, as I have said, deny that one is required to do what would have the best overall outcome on all of those occasions when the agent-centred restrictions do not forbid it, they in effect include an agent-centred prerogative of some form, although not necessarily of the very same form as I describe in Chapter Two of this book, and although the term 'agent-centred prerogative' is of course my own. For further discussion of this and related points, see the last paragraph of Chapter Two and footnote 8 of Chapter Four.

to certain important anti-consequentialist intuitions. To this extent it is on a par with agent-centred restrictions. But, as I will also argue, there is a significant asymmetry between the two agent-centred features; that is, it is much easier to identify a plausible theoretical foundation for the former than it is for the latter. Thus an agent-centred prerogative can be motivated and defended not merely by showing that it has intuitive appeal in certain cases, but also by demonstrating that there is a plausible principled rationale which underlies it. To the extent that this rationale is compelling, hybrid conceptions may, by virtue of incorporating such a prerogative, seem more attractive than consequentialist conceptions. And at the same time, the fact that it is indeed possible to provide a persuasive theoretical rationale for one departure from consequentialism will make the difficulties in providing such a rationale for agent-centred restrictions seem all the more striking, whatever the intuitive appeal of such restrictions. The upshot is that hybrid theories, intermediate between consequentialist and fully agent-centred conceptions and less familiar than either, may in the end seem preferable to both. At the very least, they will emerge as a serious alternative. Or so I hope to show.

My argument will be somewhat circuitous. I will start out, in the remainder of this chapter, by reviewing two important and influential objections to utilitarianism, each of which gives voice to a kind of intuitive uneasiness about utilitarianism which many people feel. I will try to explain how these two objections are related to each other, but I will not consider the merits of the objections or possible replies to them right away. Instead, in Chapter Two, I will sketch the outline of one parti- cular hybrid conception which is clearly capable of accommo- dating both objections. Its inclusion of an agent-centred prerogative enables the view to accommodate one of the objections, and its inclusion of what I call a 'distribution-sensi- tive' conception of the overall good enables it to accommodate the other. Once the outline of this hybrid theory is before us, I will turn in Chapter Three to an evaluation of the two objec- tions to utilitarianism which prompted the construction of the hybrid view. I will argue that even if the objections as formu- lated in the recent literature and discussed here can be answered by the utilitarian, there is nevertheless a deep, principled rationale underlying each of the two features that enable the hybrid theory sketched in Chapter Two to meet those objections. Thus even if the two objections as they stand can be rebutted, the intuitive uneasiness to which each gives voice can be provided with a more defensible principled foundation. That it may not be possible to say the same for agent-centred restrictions and the intuitive objections to which *they* respond I will argue in Chapter Four. As I have already indicated, I will try to show that although such restrictions have considerable intuitive appeal, it is surprisingly difficult to find persuasive hypotheses as to what their underlying rationale might be. This difficulty is all the more troubling in light of the fact that it *is* possible to identify such a rationale for an agent-centred prerogative, and may be seen by some as a reason for preferring a hybrid conception such as the one outlined in Chapter Two to a fully agent-centred conception. In Chapter Five I will reconsider the structure of the investigation undertaken in the first four chapters, and further examine the implications of that investigation.

Let me begin, then, by reviewing the two objections to utilitarianism to which I have alluded, and by explaining how these two criticisms, one dealing with personal integrity and the other with distributive justice, are related to each other. Williams argues that utilitarianism erodes the integrity of individuals by virtue of its strong doctrine of 'negative responsibility'. On this doctrine, one is as responsible for outcomes one fails to prevent as for outcomes one directly brings about, even when a crucial component of the outcome one fails to prevent consists of someone *else's* doing something. Thus, for example, one must abandon the projects one cares most about and strive to thwart the evil projects of others, any time doing so will avert a worse overall state of affairs. As a result of this doctrine, Williams claims, the link between one's deepest commitments and concerns, on the one hand, and one's actions, on the other hand, is thoroughly and systematically severed. Williams poses the issue as follows: 'how can a man, as a utilitarian agent, come to regard as one satisfaction among others, and a dispensable one, a project or attitude round which he has built his life, just because someone else's projects have so structured the causal scene that that is how the utilitarian sum comes out?' To require that he do this, Williams writes, 'is to alienate him in a real sense from his actions and the source of his action in his own convictions. It is to make him into a channel between the input of everyone's projects, including his own, and an output of optimific decision; but this is to neglect the extent to which *his* actions and *his* decisions have to be seen as the actions and decisions which flow from the projects and attitudes with which he is most closely identified. It is thus, in the most literal sense, an attack on his integrity.'[7]

Despite the suggestiveness of Williams's remarks, his formulation leaves obscure precisely what feature of utilitarianism is supposed to alienate the agent from his actions and hence to undermine his integrity.[8] One natural way to read him is as maintaining that utilitarianism alienates an agent from his actions by making the permissibility of the agent's devoting energy to his projects and commitments dependent on the state of the world viewed from an impersonal standpoint. If, through no fault of the agent's, things get bad enough from the impersonal standpoint, his projects become dispensable. But if it is *this* feature of utilitarianism that attacks the agent's integrity, it is doubtful that any theory but complete egoism could avoid doing so. For virtually *any* moral theory will make the permissibility of pursuing one's own projects depend at least in part on the state of the world from an impersonal standpoint. Virtually any moral view will hold that if things get bad enough from the impersonal standpoint, the agent's projects become dispensable. Different moral views do of course differ on the question of how bad things have to get from the impersonal standpoint before the agent is required to abandon his projects. But if the objection from integrity is interpreted as an objection to the in-principle dispensability of the agent's projects, then it must be regarded as a criticism of almost all non-egoistic theories,

[7] Smart and Williams, pp. 116–17.
[8] This point is also made by Nancy Davis in 'Utilitarianism and Responsibility', *Ratio* 22 (1980): 15–35, and by John Harris in 'Williams on Negative Responsibility and Integrity', *Philosophical Quarterly* 24 (1974): 265–73.

and not as an objection to which utilitarianism is distinctively vulnerable.

I believe, however, that the objection can be reconstrued in such a way that it could not be directed at all non-egoistic theories. It should be seen as arising not in response to utilitarianism's insistence on the in-principle dispensability of the agent's projects, but rather in response to the discrepancy between the way in which concerns and commitments are *naturally* generated from a person's point of view quite independently of the weight of those concerns in an impersonal ranking of overall states of affairs, and the way in which utilitarianism requires the agent to treat the concerns generated from his point of view as altogether dependent for their *moral* significance on their weight in such a ranking. In other words, utilitarianism incorporates a conception of the right which requires each agent in all cases to produce the best available outcome overall. It requires the agent to pursue his projects, commitments, and personal relationships whenever and to the extent that doing so would have the best overall outcome impersonally judged, and to neglect or abandon them whenever and to the extent that *that* would have the best overall outcome impersonally judged. Utilitarianism thus requires the agent to allocate energy and attention to the projects and people he cares most about *in strict proportion* to the value from an impersonal standpoint of his doing so, even though people typically acquire and care about their commitments quite independently of, and out of proportion to, the value that their having and caring about them is assigned in an impersonal ranking of overall states of affairs. It is *this* feature of utilitarianism which may be thought to alienate the agent 'from his actions and the source of his action in his own convictions', and thereby to undermine his integrity. So construed, the objection based on integrity could not be directed against those non-egoistic theories that do not share the utilitarian conception of the right, for they lack the feature that is now being said to generate the objection. While holding that there are circumstances in which people are required to turn their attention away from their own personal concerns, these theories do not require that agents devote energy and attention to their projects and commitments *in strict proportion* to the value from an impersonal standpoint of their doing so.

In his discussion of integrity, Williams explicitly focuses on instances when utilitarianism requires an agent to abandon his projects because 'someone else's projects have so structured the causal scene that that is how the utilitarian sum comes out'. Now while it may seem particularly intrusive that the permissibility of pursuing one's own projects and commitments should be so dependent on the projects and commitments of other people, the objection based on integrity as I am construing it does not arise specifically in response to such cases. It arises in response to the utilitarian conception of the right which requires each agent in all cases to produce the best available outcome overall. It urges that this conception of the right holds the agent's ability to permissibly pursue his own projects and plans unacceptably hostage to the state of the world viewed from an impersonal standpoint, regardless of the extent to which that state has been shaped by human activity specifically. Thus although the objection as I am construing it cannot be directed against all non-egoistic theories, it is nevertheless in this respect more general than Williams's formulation suggests. And it applies not only to utilitarianism but to every consequentialist theory. For every consequentialist theory incorporates the same conception of the right. Thus every such theory must answer the charge of alienating the agent from his actions and the source of his action in his own convictions, and hence of undermining his integrity.

What is the relation between this objection to consequentialist theories and the objection to utilitarianism based on distributive justice? Because it is concerned to maximize *total aggregate* satisfaction or utility, classical utilitarianism demands that we channel resources to the relatively well-off whenever that will lead to the required maximization. As a result, it is alleged, classical utilitarianism will frequently require us to ignore the misery of a few people and concentrate instead on increasing the pleasures of the many simply in order to maximize aggregate satisfaction. And, it is said, this is morally unacceptable. This objection to utilitarianism is a familiar one, and it may not be immediately evident how it is connected to the criticism based on integrity. The connection can be made clear by looking briefly at Rawls's argument that a failure to appreciate the separateness of persons is at the heart of classical utilitarianism's difficulties with distributive justice.

In *A Theory of Justice*, Rawls argues that the far-reaching utilitarian willingness to 'balance satisfactions and dissatisfactions between different individuals'[9] can be seen as 'the consequence of extending to society the principle of choice for one man, and then, to make this extension work, conflating all persons into one through the imaginative acts of the impartial sympathetic spectator'.[10] In view of this conflation, Rawls maintains, '[u]tilitarianism does not take seriously the distinction between persons'.[11] Elaborating, he argues that people in the hypothetical choice situation he calls 'the original position' would reject utilitarian principles of justice because those principles would require the sacrifice of some people's life prospects in order to increase the non-essential satisfactions of other people whenever that would serve to maximize total aggregate satisfaction, and because public recognition of such principles would prevent many individuals from satisfying their rational interest in securing their self-respect. In other words, utilitarianism would not be chosen by people who knew, as the parties in Rawls's original position do, that they each had some rational plan of life, plus a serious long-term interest in carrying out that plan. For as separate individuals with separate systems of ends, such people would have no comparably serious interest in maximizing total aggregate satisfaction *per se*. And so they would be unwilling to accept the sacrifice of some people's life prospects simply in order to increase that sum. Hence, Rawls says, 'if we assume that . . . the plurality of distinct persons with separate systems of ends is an essential feature of human societies, we should not expect the principles of social choice to be utilitarian'.[12]

The objection to utilitarianism based on distributive justice asserts that persons have distinct systems of ends and plans that they would not be willing (and should not always be required)

---

[9] *A Theory of Justice*, p. 24.
[10] Ibid., p. 27.
[11] Ibid., p. 27.
[12] Ibid., p. 29.

to forgo in order that maximum overall utility may be achieved. When the objection is thought of in that way, its relation to the objection from integrity becomes clear. For that objection asserts that people have certain distinct projects and commitments that they would not be willing (and should not always be required) to voluntarily abandon in order that the best overall state of affairs may be achieved. The two objections focus on two different ways of making the same supposed mistake: two different ways of failing to take sufficient account of the separateness and nature of persons. In constructing utilitarian principles of distributive justice, the supposed mistake is made by incorporating a conception of the overall good which ranks states of affairs according to the amount of total aggregate satisfaction they contain, even if a higher total of satisfaction requires the complete sacrifice of some individuals' life prospects. The resulting distributive principles, which direct that social institutions actually promote the best states of affairs so construed, will thus deny a few people the necessities of life and the prerequisites for pursuing their projects, any time their sufferings will be outweighed by the pleasures of the many in the calculus of satisfactions. In constructing principles of personal morality, the supposed mistake is made by incorporating a conception of the right that requires an agent to abandon his or her own projects and plans, any time some alternative set of activities would be productive of a better overall state of affairs.

As I have said, since the objection based on personal integrity is an objection to the conception of the right that all consequentialist theories share, this objection can be directed at all consequentialist theories. But since the objection based on distributive justice is, ultimately, an objection to the utilitarian conception of the overall good, and since different consequentialist theories have different conceptions of the overall good— that is, different principles for ranking states of affairs—the objection based on distributive justice may not be an objection to all consequentialist theories. I want to emphasize again that I will not consider until Chapter Three the question of whether the two objections are well taken: that is, of whether utilitarianism has a satisfactory reply to the objection dealing with distributive justice, and whether *any* consequentialist theory has a satisfactory reply to the objection dealing with personal integrity. Before addressing these matters I will outline a normative conception that clearly does avoid the two objections. This conception, as I have indicated, does depart from consequentialism, but not to the extent of incorporating agent-centred restrictions, and it thus occupies an intermediate position between the two most familiar types of ethical theory.

2

OUTLINE OF A NEW THEORY
OF NORMATIVE ETHICS

I will begin my characterization of the theory I have in mind by asking how one could modify a consequentialist conception in such a way as to clearly accommodate the objection dealing with personal integrity. As I have construed it, that objection arises in response to the discrepancy between the way in which concerns and commitments are naturally generated and sustained from a person's point of view quite independently of the weight of those concerns and commitments in an impersonal ranking of overall states of affairs, and the way in which the consequentialist conception of the right requires agents to allocate energy and attention to their projects and commitments in strict proportion to the weight from an impersonal standpoint of their doing so. So suppose that one were to modify a consequentialist theory (remaining neutral, for the moment, on the question *which* consequentialist theory) by changing its conception of the right, in such a way as to make it permissible for agents to devote energy and attention to their projects *out* of proportion to the weight from an impersonal standpoint of their doing so. Agents would no longer be required always to produce the best overall outcome; each agent would have the prerogative to devote energy and attention to his projects and commitments out of proportion to their weight in the impersonal calculus. Such a prerogative would be a genuinely *agent-centred* prerogative, for it would have the function of denying that what an agent is permitted to do in every situation is limited strictly to what would have the best overall outcome, impersonally judged.

I will maintain shortly that a hybrid theory which departed from consequentialism only to the extent of incorporating an

agent-centred prerogative could accommodate the objection
dealing with personal integrity. But first it is necessary to give a
fuller characterization of a plausible prerogative of this kind. To
avoid confusion, it is important to make a sharp distinction at
the outset between an agent-centred prerogative and a consequentialist dispensation to devote more attention to one's
own happiness and well-being than to the happiness and well-
being of others. Consequentialists often argue that a differential
attention to one's own concerns will in most actual circumstances have the best overall results, and that such differential
treatment of oneself is therefore required on consequentialist
grounds. Two sorts of considerations are typically appealed to
in support of this view. First, it is said that one is in a better
position to promote one's own welfare and the welfare of those
one is closest to than to promote the welfare of other people. So
an agent produces maximum good per unit of activity by focusing his efforts on those he is closest to, including himself.
Second, it is said that human nature being what it is, people
cannot function effectively at all unless they devote somewhat
more energy to promoting their own well-being than to promoting the well-being of other people. Here the appeal is no
longer to the immediate consequentialist advantages of promoting one's own well-being, but rather to the long-term
advantages of having psychologically healthy agents who are
efficient producers of the good. We find an example of the first
type of argument in Sidgwick's remark that 'each man is better
able to provide for his own happiness than for that of other
persons, from his more intimate knowledge of his own desires
and needs, and his greater opportunities of gratifying them'.[1]
Mill, in the same vein, writes that 'the occasions on which any
person (except one in a thousand) has it in his power
. . . to be a public benefactor—are but exceptional; and on these
occasions alone is he called on to consider public utility; in every
other case, private utility, the interest or happiness of some few
persons, is all he has to attend to'.[2] Sidgwick suggests an

[1] Henry Sidgwick, *The Methods of Ethics* (seventh edition) (London: Macmillan & Co.,
Ltd., 1907), p. 431.
[2] John Stuart Mill, *Utilitarianism* (Indianapolis: Bobbs-Merrill, 1957), p. 25.

argument of the second type when he says that because 'it is under the stimulus of self-interest that the active energies of most men are most easily and thoroughly drawn out', it would 'not under actual circumstances promote the universal happiness if each man were to concern himself with the happiness of others as much as with his own'.[3]

My concern here is not with the question of whether these arguments really succeed in establishing a consequentialist dispensation to devote more attention to one's own welfare than to the welfare of other people. Nor is it with the question of whether such a dispensation might provide the consequentialist with the basis for a satisfactory response to the objection dealing with personal integrity; I have already said that I will not consider the merits of possible consequentialist responses to that objection until the next chapter. At present, I wish only to stress the difference between an agent-centred prerogative and the kind of dispensation these consequentialist arguments seek to establish. The consequentialist arguments are intended to show that one may frequently be justified, from a consequentialist point of view, in devoting more energy to one's own welfare than to the welfare of others. These arguments in no way deviate from the consequentialist position that one ought always to do what would have the best outcome overall, and that one ought therefore to devote energy and attention to one's projects and commitments in strict proportion to the weight that doing so is assigned from the impersonal standpoint.[4] The arguments are simply intended, within the context of that

---

[3] *The Methods of Ethics*, p. 431.

[4] Remember that I am talking about the arguments that a standard act-consequentialist might give in favour of a dispensation to devote more attention to one's own welfare than to the welfare of other people. Defenders of other forms of consequentialism, like rule-consequentialism or motive-consequentialism, might use somewhat similar lines of argument in an attempt to defend a kind of dispensation which did in certain respects represent a departure from the strict act-consequentialist position described in the text. As I have said, I am limiting my discussion of consequentialism in this book to act-consequentialism, so I will not attempt to evaluate these other types of consequentialist arguments. It should be clear, however, that the agent-centred prerogative is also distinct from the dispensations that proponents of such views might argue on behalf of, for the agent-centred prerogative is advanced on independent grounds, and so it could, if those grounds proved compelling, be accepted even if the broadly consequentialist arguments were found wanting.

consequentialist position, to support a particular thesis about the likely relative weighting from the impersonal standpoint of attempts to promote one's own well-being and attempts to promote the well-being of others. In contrast, an agent-centred prerogative would have the function of denying that one ought always to do what would have the best outcome overall. It would deny that people ought to devote energy and attention to their projects and commitments in strict proportion to the weight from an impersonal standpoint of their doing so. It would systematically permit people, within certain limits, to devote energy and attention to their projects and commitments even if their doing so would *not* on balance promote the best outcomes overall. Whereas the consequentialist seeks to show that devoting more attention to one's own projects than to the welfare of other people is often desirable on consequentialist grounds, the function of an agent-centred prerogative would be to deny that the permissibility of devoting energy to one's projects and commitments depends on the efficacy of such activity as an instrument of overall benefit.

How, more specifically, might such a prerogative operate? One way in which it could *not* reasonably operate is by simply establishing a kind of 'protected zone' within which each agent would be permitted to do anything at all. That is, it could not reasonably function by requiring each agent to produce the best states of affairs (say) fifty per cent of the time, but releasing him from this requirement for the other fifty per cent of the time and permitting him to do anything whatsoever. This schizophrenic arrangement would, for moral purposes, divide each person into two: a perfect egoist and a perfect consequentialist. Although such a suggestion may seem too ludicrous to require discussion, it is both interesting and important to see where it goes wrong. A protected-zone prerogative would provide both too weak and too strong a guarantee of each agent's ability to take a special interest in his own projects and commitments. It would be too weak because, although it would permit each agent to devote energy and attention to his projects and commitments out of proportion to the weight in an impersonal ranking of his doing so, it would not do this in such a way as to facilitate personal integrity. Personal integrity involves a relation of consistency between an agent's values and his actions within the structure of a unified personality. And a protected-zone prerogative would undermine the unity and consistency of personality that are prerequisites for living a life of integrity.

While such a prerogative would in this respect be too weak, there are other respects in which it would be too strong. For it would allow the egoistic self to pursue whatever projects and activities it desired in complete freedom from all moral restraints. And even if one believes that a normative theory should permit each person to devote energy and attention to his projects out of proportion to the weight in an impersonal calculus of his doing so, and that it should permit the coherent integration of motivation and action within a unified personality, one can still insist that the theory should not do these things unconditionally. A person whose deepest and most powerful desire is to inflict pain on others, and who acts accordingly, may succeed in establishing a coherent personality. Here as elsewhere, coherence is not enough. I do not know whether to say that a coherent relationship between motivation and action is not enough for *personal integrity*, or alternatively, to say that coherence is enough for integrity and that therefore integrity is not enough. Can the charming and avowedly self-interested con artist live a life of integrity? Or the thoroughgoing sadist who earns a living by torturing political prisoners? Or the hard-bitten mercenary whose love of violence and adventure leads him to sell his services as a killer to the highest bidder? Perhaps; it seems to me that ordinary language pulls two ways on questions like this. But whether or not it is correct to say that such people could lead lives of integrity, one can still insist that their projects are not the sort that a moral conception must make room for. This point can be made either by saying that an agent-centred prerogative should enable each person to live a life of integrity, where integrity is understood to presuppose more than mere consistency, or by saying that it should enable each person to live a life of integrity only provided that certain further conditions are satisfied. A protected-zone prerogative would be too strong in the sense that it would place no moral restrictions on the projects and plans that the egoistic self might pursue.[5]

So in discussing the reasons for the unsuitability of the kind of prerogative I have been calling a 'protected-zone prerogative', two desiderata for a more adequate agent-centred prerogative have emerged. First, such a prerogative should not merely permit an agent to devote energy and attention to his projects out of proportion to the weight from an impersonal standpoint of his doing so, but rather it should do this in such a way as to permit the coherent integration of the agent's values and actions within the structure of a unified personality. But second, an acceptable agent-centred prerogative should place appropriate restrictions on the values and actions whose coherent integration and development it will protect.

Remember that it is the unlimited responsibility for producing optimal outcomes that consequentialism assigns to individuals which exposes the view to the objection dealing with integrity, as I have construed it. For the 'strict proportionality requirement' is a consequence of that unlimited assignment of personal responsibility. Now the protected-zone prerogative sought to accommodate personal integrity by placing limits on individual responsibility. It did so in an admittedly clumsy way: by suggesting that an agent should have unlimited responsibility for some fixed percentage of time and no responsibility for the rest of the time. Although this sort of prerogative is unacceptable, for the reasons mentioned, the underlying idea that personal integrity can be accommodated by placing a limit on responsibility is sound. Indeed, the question of how a plausible agent-centred prerogative might operate could be recast as the question how limits can best be placed on personal responsibility in such a way as to satisfy the two desiderata that the protected-zone prerogative failed to satisfy.

Non-consequentialist accounts of personal responsibility tend to rely heavily on claims that people are specially responsible for what they do, but not for what they fail to prevent. To be sure, these claims are modified to accommodate unusual

[5] But see the last two paragraphs of Chapter Three, Section I.

circumstances, but they still occupy a central position in traditional non-consequentialist analyses. As I will indicate shortly, I believe that such analyses are in general highly problematic. Before expressing my reservations about these traditional accounts, however, I want to give an indication of the way in which I think an adequate agent-centred prerogative might plausibly limit personal responsibility. If the unrestricted responsibility for producing optimal outcomes that consequentialism assigns to individuals is thought to be objectionably demanding, then the natural solution is to allow agents not to promote such outcomes when it would be unduly costly or burdensome for them to do so. On a plausible view of this kind, the answer to the question of whether an agent was required to promote the best overall outcome in a given situation would depend on the amount of good he could thereby produce (or evil he could thereby avert), and on the size of the sacrifice he would have to make in order to achieve the optimal outcome. More specifically, I believe that a plausible agent-centred prerogative would allow each agent to assign a certain proportionately greater weight to his own interests than to the interests of other people. It would then allow the agent to promote the non-optimal outcome of his choosing, provided only that the degree of its inferiority to each of the superior outcomes he could instead promote in no case exceeded, by more than the specified proportion, the degree of sacrifice necessary for him to promote the superior outcome. If all of the non-optimal outcomes available to the agent were ruled out on these grounds, then and only then would he be required to promote the best overall outcome.[6]

If a satisfactory account along these general lines could indeed be produced, I think the result would be an agent-

[6] Notice that this formulation does not represent the only way in which an agent-centred prerogative might give content to the intuitive idea of permitting agents not to promote optimal outcomes when it would be unduly burdensome for them to do so. A different kind of prerogative might allow the agent to assign some proportionately greater weight to his own interests than to the interests of other people, and then permit him to produce only those outcomes which were at least as highly-ranked as the most highly-ranked outcome he could produce consistently with the assignment of proportionately greater weight to his own interests. This version of an agent-centred prerogative would be more demanding, and to my mind less plausible, than the version described in the text.

centred prerogative of just the sort that is required.[7] Such a prerogative would obviously make it permissible for agents to devote time and energy to their projects, commitments, and personal relationships out of proportion to the weight from an impersonal standpoint of their doing so. And it would do this, moreover, in such a way as to satisfy the two desiderata that the protected-zone prerogative failed to satisfy. First, it would not divide the self into two halves, each at odds with the other. Rather, it would permit the coherent integration of one's values and actions within the structure of a unified personality, since the time and energy that one might permissibly devote to one's own projects would be woven throughout the fabric of one's life, and would not be confined to some special sphere. At the same time, however, such a prerogative would not permit one to pursue one's own projects at all costs. Thus such a prerogative would enable a normative view to accommodate personal integrity without collapsing into egoism.

What would a hybrid view that departed from consequentialism only to the extent of incorporating an agent-centred prerogative of this general type look like? First, as we have seen, people would not always be required to bring about the best state of affairs accessible to them, on such a view. Within the limits established by the principles defining the agent-centred prerogative, they could permissibly pursue their own projects. Thus the view would clearly avoid the objection dealing with personal integrity as construed in Chapter One. Since it would permit people to devote energy and attention to their projects and commitments out of proportion to the weight from the impersonal standpoint of their doing so, the view would lack the feature that generates that objection. But at the same time, it would certainly on such a view always be *permissible* for an agent to bring about the best available state of affairs. Thus there might be an agent who willingly sacrificed his own projects for

[7] In arriving at a satisfactory formulation of such a prerogative, one question that would obviously have to be faced is the question of *how much* greater weight the agent may give to his own interests than to the interests of other people. Another is the question of whether there are some sacrifices so great that they can never be morally required, no matter how high the stakes to others may be. The issues raised by these questions are certainly not neat or simple, but they are unavoidable for almost anyone whose moral outlook is neither egoist nor consequentialist.

the greater good; on this view his conduct would be supererogatory. Or there might be an agent whose project simply *was* to bring about the best state of affairs; this project would in no way be ruled out by the agent-centred prerogative, and would be entirely permissible on this view.

This last point is an important one, and it is worth emphasizing. If consequentialism is thought to erode personal integrity by requiring agents to allocate energy and attention to their projects in strict proportion to the weight *sub specie aeternitatis* of their doing so, then the natural solution is to deem it permissible, within certain limits, for agents to devote energy to their projects *out* of proportion to the weight *sub specie aeternitatis* of their doing so. But if someone *wants* to bring about the best state of affairs, either out of a supererogatory willingness to sacrifice his own projects or because bringing about the best *is* his project, there is no reason from the standpoint of personal integrity to forbid that. Such a person is surely not alienated 'from his actions and the source of his action in his own convictions'. In order to accommodate the objection from personal integrity, an agent-centred prerogative, which makes it permissible, within limits, for an agent to pursue his own projects even when they would not produce the best overall outcome impersonally judged, is sufficient. There is no need beyond that for agent-centred restrictions: no need to maintain that it is sometimes *impermissible* to produce the best state of affairs. A hybrid view that departed from consequentialism only to the extent of incorporating an agent-centred prerogative of the kind I have described would reflect this fact, since on such a view an agent could sometimes permissibly decline to bring about the best state of affairs, but would never be prohibited from doing so.[8]

[8] From the perspective of a hybrid conception, what would be the status of the obligations we are ordinarily supposed to have to keep our promises, and to protect and promote the interests of people to whom we stand in certain special relations (children, spouses, benefactors, and so on)? Clearly hybrid conceptions, like consequentialist conceptions, would not hold that one must fulfil such obligations even if by not doing so one could produce a better outcome overall. On the other hand, hybrid conceptions, unlike consequentialist conceptions, would often *permit* agents to keep their promises and to promote the interests of people to whom they stand in special relations, even if by not doing so they could produce better overall outcomes. For hybrid conceptions permit people to devote energy and attention to their projects, commitments, and

From the perspective of a hybrid theory of this kind, the traditional non-consequentialist doctrine that duties not to harm are stronger than duties to help would be comprehensible only up to a very limited point. Consider two parallel cases. In the first case, an agent can avert an undesirable overall outcome if he simply refrains from harming some person. In the second case, the agent will avert the same amount of evil if he helps some person. Now in many parallel cases of this kind, where harming someone and failing to help someone will lead to equally undesirable outcomes overall, an agent-centred pre-rogative of the kind I have described might in fact require that the agent refrain from harming but not that he help. For, in many cases of this kind, even if both overall outcomes would be equally undesirable, a demand to avert the first would leave the agent free to pursue a wide range of alternative activities, while a demand to avert the second would severely restrict the options open to him.[9] Thus in many cases of this kind, a demand of the first sort would be much less burdensome to the agent than a demand of the second sort. However, traditional non-con-sequentialist analyses of responsibility typically go much further than this. They ordinarily maintain that, in parallel

personal relationships out of proportion to the weight in an impersonal calculus of their doing so. Now in addition, hybrid conceptions might ordinarily require agents to keep their promises and fulfil those special obligations incurred as a result of their voluntary activity *unless* by not doing so they would produce a better overall outcome. For, it might be said, when one makes a promise or voluntarily acts in such a way as to incur a special obligation, one ordinarily forfeits the prerogative to give one's own interests more weight than the relevant interests of those to whom one becomes bound. Hence a final characterization of an acceptable agent-centred prerogative might include a proviso that one may ordinarily neglect voluntarily incurred obligations only if doing so would be in the general interest, and not if it would simply be in one's own interest. Notice that such a proviso, though restrictive, could hardly be said to undermine one's integrity, since it would apply only to obligations incurred as a result of one's voluntary activity.

[9] For related discussions, see Jonathan Bennett, '"Whatever the Consequences"', *Analysis* 26 (1966): 83–102; P. J. Fitzgerald, 'Acting and Refraining', *Analysis* 27 (1967): 133–9; Richard Trammel, 'Saving Life and Taking Life', *Journal of Philosophy* 72 (1975): 131–7; Carolyn Morillo, 'Doing, Refraining, and the Strenuousness of Morality', *American Philosophical Quarterly* 14 (1977): 29–39; Michael Tooley, 'A Defense of Abortion and Infanticide', in *The Problem of Abortion*, J. Feinberg, ed. (Belmont, California: Wadsworth, 1973): 51–91. The papers by Bennett and Trammel may also be found, along with a number of other relevant essays, in *Killing and Letting Die*, a very useful anthology edited by Bonnie Steinbock (Englewood Cliffs, New Jersey: Prentice-Hall, 1980).

cases of this kind, the duty not to harm is stronger than the duty
to help even if both requirements are equally burdensome for
the agent. Indeed, such accounts maintain that the duty not to
harm is *in general* at least somewhat stronger than the duty to
help, and that it therefore at least sometimes wins out in *conflicts*
between the two duties, even when it is clear that the *best* overall outcome would be achieved by inflicting a harm. As an illus-
tration consider a third case. Here an agent has two choices. He
can refrain from harming some person, but if he does so then
greater harm will befall other people, and he will be unable to
help them. He can instead help the others, but to do this he will
have to harm the first person. The overall outcome of his not
harming would here be worse than the overall outcome of his
helping. Yet typical non-consequentialist accounts maintain
that, in at least some cases of just this kind, the agent must
refrain from harming. For these views, in other words, the duty
not to harm constitutes an agent-centred restriction.[10]

   Thus, for example, some people argue as follows. If you can
either prevent the murder of one innocent person or the murder
of five innocent people, it is rational to prevent the murder of the
five, since you owe only a duty of positive aid to all six potential
victims, and if you can either provide more or less positive aid, it
is rational to provide more. But if *you* would have to murder one
innocent person in order to prevent the murder of five by
someone else, then you must not do so. Why? Because the duty
not to inflict harm oneself is much stronger than the duty to
prevent harm. The problem with this claim is that, in the
absence of some independent account of the source and basis of
these duties, it fails to provide a genuine answer to the question
it purports to address. It answers the question why a person
may not commit one harm to prevent five identical harms by
saying that one's duty not to commit harm is stronger than
one's duty to prevent still greater harm. But *why* is the one duty
stronger than the other? Until that question is answered, the
appeal to duty is hardly more informative than a claim that one
must not commit one harm to prevent five identical harms

---

[10] See, for example, Philippa Foot, 'The Problem of Abortion and the Doctrine of
Double Effect', *Oxford Review* 5 (1967): 5–15. This paper is also reprinted in Steinbock,
pp. 156–65.

because one must not commit one harm to prevent five identical harms. It only creates an illusion of being more informative by trading on some primitive picture of negative and positive duties as larger and smaller metaphysical entities, the larger being more weighty and hence naturally more influential.

Now as I have said, certain well-defined considerations would lead hybrid views to agree that the duty not to harm is stronger than the duty to prevent harm in certain pairs of cases: when harming and failing to prevent harm would both lead to equally undesirable outcomes overall, but not harming would be less burdensome to the agent than preventing harm. As we have seen, these are considerations about the desirability of allowing agents not to avert non-optimal outcomes if it would be very costly for them to do so, in order that they may be permitted to devote ample attention to their own projects and plans. But these considerations do not support the contention that agents *must* not inflict harms that will produce *optimal* outcomes overall. These considerations do not support agent-centred restrictions. Someone who wants to claim that one must not commit one harm to prevent still greater harms because the duty not to harm is stronger than the duty to prevent harm, must give some sort of explanation of the source of *this* kind of differential strength. Pending such an explanation, hybrid views are not embarrassed, and agent-centred restrictions are not supported, by the allegedly unequal strengths of the duty not to harm and the duty to prevent harm.

In Chapter One I argued that the criticism of utilitarianism based on personal integrity and the criticism based on distributive justice focus on two different ways in which utilitarianism allegedly fails to take sufficient account of the separateness and nature of persons. Since the objection dealing with integrity focuses on the utilitarian conception of the right which requires each agent in all cases to produce the best outcome overall, this objection can, as I argued, be directed at every consequentialist theory. For every consequentialist theory takes the same view of right action. Now an agent-centred prerogative of the kind I have described operates by scaling down the individual's responsibility for producing optimal outcomes, and it could be used to transform any consequentialist theory into a hybrid theory clearly capable of accommodating the objection dealing with integrity.

Of course, however, different hybrid conceptions incorporate different conceptions of the overall good; that is, they rank states of affairs from best to worst in different ways. And depending on what ranking principles they incorporate, different hybrid conceptions may be more or less responsive to the criticism directed at utilitarianism's account of distributive justice. For as I argued earlier, that criticism is ultimately directed at the way in which utilitarianism orders states of affairs from best to worst. And since different consequentialist conceptions have different principles for ordering states of affairs, the objection from justice may be unlike the objection from integrity in not applying equally to every version of consequentialism. There may be a consequentialist conception whose principle for ranking overall states of affairs is responsive to distributive concerns. If so, then the hybrid view that departs from that conception only to the extent of incorporating an agent-centred prerogative of the sort I have described would appear to have a special claim on our attention, for it would appear to be a likely candidate for a view that could accommodate *both* objections without incorporating agent-centred restrictions.

I believe that there are in fact a number of consequentialist conceptions capable of accommodating the objection based on distributive justice. The first one that I will discuss is a view whose central features were described some years ago by T. M. Scanlon.[11] This view identifies a hierarchy of levels of well-being, measured in terms of a standard which is to some extent independent of the tastes, preferences, and states of consciousness of the individuals whose well-being is being assessed, and which is in that sense objective. The view identifies the best state of affairs from among a set as the one that moves as many people as high up as possible in the hierarchy of well-being. In other words, the view uses a 'lexical' principle for ranking overall states of affairs. Given two states of affairs (in which, for simplicity, population is held constant), the better state of

[11]See Scanlon, 'Rawls' Theory of Justice', *University of Pennsylvania Law Review* 121 (1973): 1020–69.

affairs is the one that maximizes the position of the worst-off group. If the two states of affairs are identical in this respect, the better state of affairs is the one that minimizes the number of people in the worst-off group (by relocating them upward). If the two states of affairs are identical in both of these respects, then the better state of affairs is the one that maximizes the position of the next worst-off group, and so on.[12] Like other consequentialist conceptions, this theory then simply directs agents to bring about the best state of affairs available to them. Scanlon writes:

The modified utilitarian theory I have in mind here would be based on a hierarchy of levels of well-being measured in terms of some neutral standard such as Rawls's primary social goods. The goal of the theory (the standard by which acts and institutions are to be appraised) is to move as many people as high up in this ranking as possible, with the greatest importance to be set on increasing (and on not decreasing) the well-being of those who at a given time enjoy the lowest standard of well-being.[13]

This view, which I will call 'pluralistic lexical consequentialism', differs sharply from traditional utilitarian conceptions. For one thing, it does not identify a person's good with pleasurable states of consciousness or other presumed psychological quantities. This rejection of hedonism follows naturally from the rejection of 'dominant-end' conceptions of human motivation and deliberation.[14] A dominant-end theorist believes that in order for rational choice among apparently heterogenous options ever to be possible, there must be a common deliberative denominator: a single overriding end (e.g., pleasure), the achievement of which is the goal of all rational action, as a means to which all other things ought rationally to be appraised, and to which, in consequence, all other ends are rationally subservient. It is easy to see that if one

---

[12] David Lewis has pointed out that, while this provides a clear enough account of how to tell which of two states of affairs is the better one, it provides no account of how, on a lexical view, to combine these judgements with probability estimates to yield judgements about expectable value. The most natural response is that this should be done lexically too: first maximize the expectable position of the worst off, if that is equal of the next worst off, and so forth.

[13] 'Rawls' Theory of Justice', p. 1054.

[14] The ideas expressed in the remainder of this paragraph are due entirely to Rawls. See sections 60–6 and 83–4 of *A Theory of Justice*, and also Scanlon's helpful discussion in 'Rawls' Theory of Justice', especially pp. 1028–9 and 1051–3.

holds a dominant-end view of deliberation, it becomes tempting to identify the good with the dominant end. If, on the other hand, one does not believe that there exists any dominant end, one may be drawn not only to alternative accounts of rational deliberation, but also toward more pluralistic conceptions of the good. Pluralistic lexical consequentialism, as I conceive it, views human ends as irreducibly heterogeneous. And it agrees with Rawls that '[h]uman good is heterogeneous because the aims of the self are heterogeneous'.[15] A person's good, on this view, 'is determined by what is for him the most rational long-term plan of life given reasonably favorable circumstances'.[16] Different plans are rational for different people and, moreover, no formal principles of rationality are deemed capable of selecting a unique rational plan for each individual person. In order to make a choice from among those plans not ruled out by the formal principles, a person has no choice but to strive for self-understanding: to weigh the relative strength of his various concerns and to estimate the relative value he ascribes to alternative pursuits. This is, of course, the account of a person's good given by Rawls, and I conceive pluralistic lexical consequentialism as incorporating this account rather than the hedonistic account relied on by some versions of classical utilitarianism.

Now it is true that not all versions of the classical view are overtly hedonistic. Some versions identify a person's good not with pleasurable states of consciousness but rather with the satisfaction of his preferences, and 'satisfaction', in these accounts, is not understood as referring to a kind of feeling.[17] However, there remain crucial differences between pluralistic lexical consequentialism, as I conceive it, and utilitarianism even of this non-hedonistic sort. First, the two views still rely on different conceptions of the individual good, for the idea that the good for a person consists in his carrying out a rational plan of life is not the same as the idea that it consists in the maxi-

[15] *A Theory of Justice*, p. 554.

[16] Ibid., pp. 92–3.

[17] Rawls argues in 'Social Unity and Primary Goods' (in *Utilitarianism and Beyond*, Amartya Sen and Bernard Williams, eds. (Cambridge University Press, 1982)) that some such accounts of the individual good may nevertheless be implicitly hedonistic.

mized satisfaction of his preferences. This first difference is responsible for a second: given their differing accounts of the individual good, the two views quite naturally regard different standards as the appropriate ones on which to base those interpersonal comparisons of well-being which are necessary for the ranking of overall states of affairs. For the utilitarian, the appropriate standard is one which provides an indication of the extent to which different individuals' preferences are satisfied. Pluralistic lexical consequentialism, by contrast, relies as I have already said on a standard which is not sensitive exclusively to the states of consciousness *or* the preferences of the individuals whose well-being is being compared, and which is in that sense objective.[18] The appropriate standard, on this view, is one which provides an indication of the extent to which different individuals' needs and interests are met, with different human needs and interests deemed to have varying degrees of urgency, given the regulative assumption that a person's good consists in successfully carrying out a rational plan of life. In other words, that general conception of the good provides a standard relative to which some human interests can be judged more important than others. And an adequate measure of well-being is then thought to be one which constitutes a reasonable indicator of the extent to which these differentially important interests are met. The precise formulation of such a measure is obviously a matter of the first importance for pluralistic lexical consequentialism, as it is for utilitarianism and other moral views as well, but it is not a matter that I will attempt to deal with here. I wish only to stress the difference between the kind of measure the utilitarian regards as appropriate and the kind of measure that the pluralistic lexical consequentialist favours, and to suggest that this difference is rooted in a deeper disagreement about the nature of the human good. There is also a third difference between the two views. Whereas classical utilitarianism even of the non-hedonistic kind ranks states of affairs according to the amount of total utility they contain, pluralistic lexical consequentialism incorporates a *distribution-*

[18] For discussions of subjective and objective standards of well-being, see T. M. Scanlon, 'Preference and Urgency', *Journal of Philosophy* 72 (1975): 655–69, and Rawls, 'Social Unity and Primary Goods'.

sensitive conception of the overall good; its rankings of states of affairs, in other words, are directly affected by the ways in which benefits and burdens are distributed within those states of affairs.

In each of the three respects just mentioned, pluralistic lexical consequentialism is closer to Rawls's Difference Principle, which incorporates the same conception of the individual good, has a lexical structure, and relies on 'primary goods' as an objective standard for interpersonal comparisons, than it is to utilitarianism. And though the theory is certainly problematic in some ways, it does appear to avoid the objection to utilitarianism based on distributive justice. For it would never require us to ignore the misery of a few and concentrate instead on increasing the pleasures of the many in order that total aggregate satisfaction or utility might be maximized. Moreover, pluralistic lexical consequentialism is not the only imaginable form of consequentialism with a distribution-sensitive principle for ranking overall states of affairs. There might, for example, be a view called 'hedonistic lexical consequentialism', which combined a traditional hedonistic account of an individual's good with a lexical principle for ranking overall states of affairs. One can also imagine hedonistic and pluralistic variants of a view that might be called 'egalitarian consequentialism', according to which the best overall states of affairs were (very roughly) the ones in which people's levels of well-being, hedonistically or pluralistically construed, were most nearly equal. Additionally, there might be views which combined a preference-satisfaction account of the individual good with either a lexical or an egalitarian ranking principle. All of these views might well be able to avoid the objection based on distributive justice.

To my mind, however, all of the distribution-sensitive forms of consequentialism mentioned so far seem implausibly rigid. The lexical variants, for example, would appear to require that the worst-off group's level of well-being must be raised just slightly, even if instead those who were nearly as badly-off could be raised substantially. And the egalitarian variants would appear to require that given a choice between a situation in which everyone is very badly-off but equally so, and a situation in which everyone is very well-off but slight inequalities exist, we must always choose the former.

To my mind, the most plausible distribution-sensitive form of consequentialism is one which is in all other respects like the pluralistic lexical variant, but which abandons the strict lexical ranking principle in favour of a more flexible 'distributive' principle, according to which the lower a person's level of relative well-being is, the greater the weight that is given to benefiting him. Thus on this view, which I shall call 'distributive consequentialism', the claims of those who are worse off often take priority over the claims of those who are better off, even if a higher total utility could be achieved by benefiting the latter. But although this view gives *much greater weight* to benefiting those who are worst-off, it does not give *absolute priority* to doing so. And so it might hold that, as between one state of affairs in which the worst-off group was benefited slightly, and another state of affairs in which those who were nearly as badly off were benefited substantially, the latter was, other things equal, the better state of affairs.

Obviously, this provides only the sketchiest kind of characterization of distributive consequentialism. For one thing, this characterization inherits much of the incompleteness of the account of pluralistic lexical consequentialism. Thus, for example, nothing specific has been said about the nature of the objective standard of well-being relied upon, about how this standard is applied, about how questions of population are handled, and so on. And in addition, distributive consequentialism has difficulties of its own. Its principle for ranking overall states of affairs is much less neat and clear than a lexical principle; questions arise, on the distributive view, about *how much* greater weight should be given to benefiting those at the relatively lower levels of well-being, and these questions are enormously complex and messy. However, it is worth remembering that a rigid lexical ordering of claims is 'neat' at the cost of being implausible. Here, as in many other parts of moral philosophy, one must choose between simplicity and credibility. And, despite the sketchiness of the characterization of distributive consequentialism, it still seems possible to say with some confidence that the view has the resources to avoid the objection to utilitarianism based on distributive justice, as formulated in Chapter One. For it would never require that we ignore the misery of the worst-off and concentrate instead on multiplying the pleasures of the well-off simply in order to maximize total aggregate satisfaction. There are indeed many important problems that would have to be addressed in a full characterization of distributive consequentialism. But many of these problems also arise for other accounts of justice, and what seems undeniable about distributive consequentialism is that it has the ability to make good sense of distributive concerns, yet at the same time lacks the absolutist rigidity of lexical or egalitarian consequentialism.

On the assumption that these observations are not too far off the mark, let us now consider a moral conception that departs from distributive consequentialism only to the extent of incorporating an agent-centred prerogative of the sort earlier discussed. I will call this conception 'the distributive hybrid', with apologies for the evident gracelessness of the term. Because of its agent-centred prerogative, the distributive hybrid can accommodate criticisms of consequentialism dealing with personal integrity. Because of its distribution-sensitive principle for ranking overall states of affairs, it can accommodate the objection to utilitarianism based on distributive justice.[19]

This last point requires some elaboration. For the distributive hybrid, by virtue of incorporating an agent-centred prerogative, may appear to be exclusively a theory of personal morality, designed to indicate what individual agents may and must do and not do. The problem of distributive justice, by contrast, typically arises as a problem of institutional policy and

[19] I do not mean to claim that the distributive hybrid is the only hybrid conception that can accommodate these two objections. There may be views that differ from the distributive hybrid, either by incorporating a different kind of agent-centred prerogative, or a different distribution-sensitive principle for ranking overall states of affairs, which can also accommodate the two objections. I am simply focusing on the distributive hybrid because it seems to me the most plausible hybrid view. As I will emphasize in Chapter Three, the rationales that I offer there for an agent-centred prerogative and a distribution-sensitive ranking principle do presuppose that those devices take forms which make them responsive to the objections dealing with integrity and justice, but they do not presuppose the particular versions of the two devices that are incorporated into the moral conception I am calling 'the distributive hybrid'. Thus someone who found those rationales compelling might nevertheless accept a different kind of agent-centred prerogative or a different distribution-sensitive principle for ranking states of affairs.

social choice. It arises as a problem about how governmental institutions are required to operate. Since utilitarianism uses just one principle to evaluate both governmental policies and individual acts (both must maximize total satisfaction), it is clearly committed to a certain account of distributive justice. And since distributive consequentialism also uses just one principle to evaluate both governmental policies and individual acts, it too is clearly committed to an account of distributive justice. So there is no difficulty in understanding the claim that distributive consequentialism can accommodate the objection to utilitarianism based on distributive justice. But since the distributive hybrid seems to address itself exclusively to individual agents, it may seem to be altogether silent on questions of governmental policy. How then can *it* be said to accommodate the objection to utilitarianism based on distributive justice?

This question calls attention to the fact that the relations between principles of personal morality and principles for the appraisal of social institutions are more complicated on typical non-consequentialist views than they are on consequentialist views. If one knows what principle a consequentialist uses to evaluate individual actions, then one also knows what principle he uses to evaluate social policy. This is not true with a non-consequentialist, for although the principles of personal and institutional morality are certainly closely related on any plausible non-consequentialist view, they need not be identical. Thus the distributive hybrid, when fully developed, is *not* exclusively an account of personal morality, but it is not possible to simply 'read off' its institutional principles from its personal principles. The question of what its institutional principles are is a complicated one, and I will not try to resolve it here, since any resolution would require a treatment of issues well beyond the scope of my project. What I will do instead is to give an indication of what the range of possibilities seems to be, and to argue that no matter which of these accounts is correct, the distributive hybrid remains invulnerable to the objection to utilitarianism based on distributive justice. If that is right, then it is fair to claim that the distributive hybrid can accommodate that objection even if the question of which account of its institutional principles is correct is left open.

At one end of the spectrum, what might be said about the

distributive hybrid's institutional principles is that they are
identical to those of distributive consequentialism. For, it might
be said, the distributive hybrid departs from distributive consequentialism only to the extent of incorporating an agent-
centred prerogative, allowing *individuals* to devote energy and
attention to their projects out of proportion to the weight from
an impersonal standpoint of their doing so. And since governmental institutions are not individual persons, the distributive
hybrid's principles of right for institutions do not incorporate an
agent-centred prerogative, but rather remain identical to the
principles of distributive consequentialism. In other words, the
distributive hybrid accepts distributive consequentialism's
institutional principles, for it rejects the consequentialist
account of the right only in so far as that account is thought to
undermine personal integrity. Governments must still do what
is best overall, distributively construed.

An intermediate position might be that the distributive
hybrid's institutional principles differ from those of distributive
consequentialism in just the way that the personal principles of
the former differ from those of the latter. On this view, a
government *may* always do what would have the best outcome
overall, but within certain limits it may instead choose to
concentrate on doing what would have the best results for its
own citizens. In other words, governments have the prerogative
to devote somewhat more weight to the interests of their own
citizens than to the interests of other people. This, it might be
said, is the natural reflection on the governmental level of the
fact that each of the individual citizens of any state has the
prerogative to give somewhat more weight to his own interests
than to the interests of other people.[20]

At the other end of the spectrum, it might be said that since
each individual has the prerogative to devote somewhat more

[20]Compare T. Nagel:

> There is some public analogue to the individual's right to lead his own life free of
> the constant demand to promote the best overall results, but it appears in the
> relations of states to one another rather than in their relations to their citizens:
> states can remain neutral in external disputes, and can legitimately favor their
> own populations—though not at any cost whatever to the rest of the world.

('Ruthlessness in Public Life', in *Mortal Questions* (Cambridge University Press, 1979),
p. 84.)

weight to his own interests than to the interests of other people, it is permissible for a group of people, if they so desire, to establish a government which is not supposed to devote itself exclusively to promoting optimal results, either for its own citizens or for everyone. In other words, individuals may choose to exercise their prerogatives by establishing a government to serve as an instrument for achieving certain of their own legitimate ends, and they may instruct that government to act in whatever way they wish, provided that in so doing they do not exceed the bounds of their prerogatives by giving more weight to their own interests than they are entitled to.

These three possibilities are not exhaustive, but they do seem to me representative of the spectrum of possible positions. Any one of them would have to be developed in considerably more detail before its merits could be finally assessed. What I wish to stress, however, is that none of these positions would make the distributive hybrid vulnerable to the objection to utilitarianism dealing with distributive justice. For that objection, as I have said, arises ultimately in response to the utilitarian conception of the overall good, which ranks states of affairs according to the amount of total satisfaction they contain. And the distributive hybrid's rejection of that conception of the overall good is unequivocal. Its institutional principles, whatever they may be, rely on the distributive principle for ranking overall states of affairs. Thus none of the possible institutional principles would require that some people's life prospects be sacrificed in order to increase the non-essential satisfactions of other people whenever that would serve to maximize total aggregate satisfaction. For they all reject the conception of the overall good which leads utilitarianism to require just that.

Thus it seems fair to say that the distributive hybrid does indeed accommodate the objection based on distributive justice as well as the objection based on personal integrity. And it does not incorporate agent-centred restrictions in order to accommodate justice any more than it does to accomodate integrity. This point needs to be emphasized, for someone might think that the idea of ranking overall states of affairs in such a way as to give greater weight to the claims of those whose level of well-being is relatively low, which is built into the distributive hybrid in order to satisfy distributional considerations, does in fact smuggle in such restrictions. What this idea shows, however, is not that the distributive hybrid incorporates agent-centred restrictions, but rather that distributive considerations can be accommodated without such restrictions. For, as we have seen, the distributive hybrid takes the view that there is a way of ranking overall states of affairs impersonally such that it is always permissible to produce the best available state of affairs so characterized. And, as I have said, agent-centred restrictions are restrictions on action which have the effect of denying that there is *any* non-agent-relative principle for ranking overall states of affairs such that it is always permissible to produce the best available state of affairs so characterized. An agent-centred restriction would thus prohibit certain actions even though they would produce the best state of affairs distributively defined. It might, for example, prohibit the infliction of harm even in circumstances where harming someone was necessary to produce the best overall outcome distributively construed. It is a great irony in the recent history of ethics that many people who have criticized utilitarianism for allowing the more serious interests of a few to be sacrificed to the less serious interests of the many whenever that would maximize total aggregate satisfaction have themselves turned to moral conceptions that include agent-centred restrictions as an alternative, rather than to more sophisticated forms of consequentialism. For the conceptual distinction to which such restrictions respond is not the distinction between more and less serious human interests, but rather the distinction between what would have the best overall outcome impersonally judged and what a person may permissibly do. Even if the best state of affairs is taken to be the one in which the fewest people have their serious interests violated or neglected, a fully agent-centred conception will deny that it is always permissible to produce the best state of affairs so characterized. There may, for all I've said so far, be a plausible rationale for agent-centred restrictions, but their function is not to express the idea that some interests are more urgent than others, and they are not needed to accommodate the objection to utilitarianism based on distributive justice, as I have been construing it.

Before concluding this chapter, it is important to forestall a possible confusion. As we have seen, the distributive hybrid always allows individuals to do what would have the best outcome overall. The possibility has also been raised that its institutional principles may always *require* governments to do what would have the best outcome overall. It is thus a consequence of the view that it may sometimes be permissible for an individual, or perhaps even obligatory for a government, to force a person to do something that the person would not be required to do voluntarily. Now it might be thought that, in the end, this feature of the distributive hybrid undermines its ability to accommodate the objection dealing with personal integrity. For in circumstances where an agent would not be required to neglect his own projects in order to produce a better overall state of affairs, it might nevertheless be permissible for a second agent to force the first to abandon his projects, if by so doing the second agent would produce the best overall outcome that was available to him. Moreover, it might be said, if the distributive hybrid really did require governments always to produce the best states of affairs they could produce, that would presumably mean that it required them to systematically force individuals to in turn produce the best states of affairs *they* could produce, and hence to devote energy and attention to their projects and plans in strict proportion to the value from an impersonal standpoint of their doing so. And, it might be said, it is precisely the requirement that individuals do this that gives rise to the objection dealing with integrity. The agent-centred prerogative was thought to eliminate this 'strict proportionality requirement', but a requirement that governments always do what would have the best outcome overall would clearly nullify the effects of the prerogative. For it would mean that even if the distributive hybrid did not directly require individuals to allocate energy and attention to their projects and commitments in strict proportion to the weight from an impersonal standpoint of such activity, it nevertheless required governments to force them to do so.

This line of thought is doubly erroneous. In the first place, the objection to consequentialism, both as formulated by Williams and as I have been construing it, maintains that the consequentialist conception of the right systematically violates the integrity of all agents. Now even if the distributive hybrid did require governments always to produce the best outcomes, it still would not follow that it required them to systematically force all agents to produce optimal outcomes. For from the fact that it would have the best overall outcome for some agent to abandon his projects and pursue an alternative course of action, it does not follow that it would be best overall for someone else to force the agent to abandon his projects; the costs of using force need to be taken into account, and they are ordinarily considerable. Thus it would not even follow from a requirement that governments produce optimal outcomes, still less does it follow from the provision that individuals *may* produce optimal outcomes, that the distributive hybrid requires that all agents be systematically forced to do things that would undermine their integrity.

In the second place, a central feature of the objection to consequentialism, both as formulated by Williams and as I have been construing it, is precisely its insistence that the theory violates the integrity of agents by virtue of what it *directly* requires them to do. And even if the distributive hybrid sometimes permits individuals or requires governments to force particular people to do things that will undermine their integrity, it cannot be said even on these occasions that the conception violates the integrity of agents by virtue of what it directly requires them to do. What the distributive hybrid does do, on these occasions and more generally, is to permit individuals (and perhaps require governments) to harm a person if that is necessary in order to minimize overall weighted harms and produce the best available state of affairs. Sometimes the harms thus permitted (or required) may violate the victim's integrity; sometimes they may be even more serious. And while it may indeed be thought an objectionable form of victimization for an institution or individual to harm someone in order to minimize overall weighted harms, that is a different objection than the objection to consequentialism dealing with personal integrity. Consequentialist conceptions, like hybrid conceptions, do of course permit the infliction of such harms, and those who accept agent-centred restrictions do of course regard this as objectionable. But in addition, as we have seen, consequentialism is thought by some to systematically violate the integrity of all agents simply by virtue of what it directly requires them to do. And it is this additional objection that an agent-centred prerogative of the sort I have described clearly enables hybrid conceptions to avoid. Now as I have emphasized, it may, for all that has been said so far, be possible for the consequentialist to rebut the objection dealing with integrity without accepting an agent-centred prerogative. This question will be considered in Chapter Three. By the same token, there may, for all that has been said so far, be reason to reject the idea that it is permissible to harm one person in order to minimize overall weighted harms, and so to accept agent-centred restrictions. This question will be addressed in Chapter Four. All that should be evident at this point is that the agent-centred prerogative, by itself, does indeed enable the distributive hybrid to clearly avoid the objection dealing with integrity as I have been understanding it.

I am acutely aware that I have not presented anything approaching a complete normative conception in this chapter. I have tried only to sketch the outline of such a conception, and perhaps even this description of what I have done is overstated, suggesting a kind of completeness that I have not attempted or achieved. After all, only partial accounts have been offered of the distributive hybrid's two most distinctive features, its agent-centred prerogative and its distributive principle for evaluating states of affairs. And because of this we are left with only a general and largely intuitive idea of how the theory might operate, with its application to many particular cases remaining as yet indeterminate.

It is worth noting that incompleteness of this sort is not uncommon in characterizations of the more familiar moral conceptions. For example, accounts of agent-centred restrictions in the literature are often incomplete, leaving open, for example, the question of when exactly the restrictions may be overridden to produce a good outcome or avoid a bad one.[21] And, as I noted in Chapter One, fully agent-centred concep-

[21] See, for example, Robert Nozick, *Anarchy, State, and Utopia* (New York: Basic Books, 1974), p. 30n.

tions are also committed to an agent-centred prerogative of some form, but the task of fully characterizing the relevant kind of prerogative is usually left unfinished. Even if it is common, of course, that is not to say that incompleteness of this kind is positively desirable. But I believe that the admittedly unfinished account of the distributive hybrid that I have presented here is sufficient for the purposes of the project I have undertaken in this book. My aim in sketching the distributive hybrid has been to show that its two salient structural features clearly enable it to avoid certain prima-facie objections to utilitarianism, just as there are other intuitive objections to utilitarianism to which agent-centred restrictions are responsive. Now the incompleteness in typical accounts of such restrictions does not prevent us from grasping their intuitive appeal, or from seeing in a general way how they are supposed to function. And similarly, I believe that even though the accounts of the agent-centred prerogative and the distributive principle offered here have been incomplete, enough has been said to show that these devices, characterized along the lines I have suggested, do indeed enable the distributive hybrid to avoid the objections dealing with justice and integrity as I have been construing them. In subsequent chapters, I will go on to argue that there is an important asymmetry between such devices and agent-centred restrictions: although both are responsive to anti-utilitarian intuitions, it is much easier to identify a plausible theoretical motivation for the former than it is for the latter. If my argument is persuasive, then the task of trying to complete the account of the distributive hybrid may come to seem worthwhile. But it is the motivational investigation and not the comprehensive characterization of the distributive hybrid which will occupy my attention in the remainder of the book.

3

THE INDEPENDENCE AND DISTINCTNESS OF THE PERSONAL POINT OF VIEW

THE aim of this chapter is to explore the considerations underlying an agent-centred prerogative and the considerations underlying a distribution-sensitive conception of the overall good.

I

I will begin by investigating the motivation for an agent-centred prerogative, a prerogative to devote attention to one's projects out of proportion to the weight in the impersonal calculus of one's doing so. In conducting this investigation, I will be assuming that the prerogative has some form that makes it responsive to the objection dealing with integrity, but I will not be assuming that it must have the particular form sketched in the last chapter. It may be wondered how this limited lack of specificity in the investigation may affect the conclusions that can legitimately be drawn from it. I will return to this question at the end of the section, but until then I will put it aside.

I will begin the investigation of the motivation for a prerogative by re-examinining the objection dealing with integrity: by considering possible responses to this objection and the implications of the responses.

Broadly speaking, there are two options which the consequentialist has in responding to the objection. First, he can deny the charge that consequentialism systematically undermines personal integrity. Or second, he can concede that the charge is accurate but deny that it constitutes a weighty objection to his theory. I want to consider responses of both kinds, starting off with some instances of the first type. One response of this sort is to suggest that if indeed integrity is an important value, then a consequentialist theory can treat it as one of the goods to be promoted. Although requiring agents always to produce the best overall state of affairs, such a theory can rank states of affairs at least in part according to the 'amount' of integrity they contain. Thus whatever may be true of some of the simpler forms of consequentialism, a more complicated theory of this kind would not be generally or systematically destructive of personal integrity. Although there might be particular occasions on which it would require individuals to sacrifice their own integrity in order to produce the best overall states of affairs, it would not ignore the importance of integrity as one value among others.

As it stands, this reply is inadequate. For, as I have stressed, the objection dealing with integrity does not arise in response to a particular consequentialist conception of the overall good, but rather in response to the consequentialist conception of the right, which requires agents to devote energy to their projects in strict proportion to the weight from the impersonal standpoint of their doing so. And even a version of consequentialism like the one described would include this 'strict proportionality requirement' as a feature of its conception of the right, thus apparently vitiating its identification of integrity as a goal to be promoted. For simply by virtue of its insistence on the strict proportionality requirement, even this form of consequentialism would appear to be vulnerable to the objection from integrity in its strongest form: vulnerable, in other words, to the charge that it systematically undermines the integrity of *all* agents.

As a first step toward the development of a more persuasive rebuttal of this charge, the consequentialist may press for a detailed account of the process by which the strict proportionality requirement is thought to undermine the integrity of the individual agent. It would seem that in order for a person's integrity to be threatened by consequentialism, the person would at the very least have to be *aware* of the strict propor-

tionality requirement. For if he were unaware of the requirement, the mere fact that there was such a requirement could
hardly serve to sever the connection between the agent's values
and his actions, or to prevent him from seeing his actions and
decisions 'as the actions and decisions which flow from the
projects and attitudes with which he is most closely identified'.
Thus integrity is threatened, if at all, only when the agent
regards his projects as altogether dependent for their moral and
practical significance on their weight in an impersonal ranking
of overall states of affairs, while simultaneously caring about
them independently of, and out of proportion to, the weight that
his having and caring about them carries in such a ranking.

Once this is conceded, however, the consequentialist may
deny that his theory includes any general requirement that
people be aware of the strict proportionality requirement, or
that they regard their projects and plans in any fixed way. As
ordinarily understood, it may be said, consequentialism is a
doctrine about the rightness and wrongness of actions, and not
about the beliefs, attitudes, or motivations that people should
have. In so far as there is a consequentialist view about these
other matters, it must surely be the view that people should
have whatever beliefs, attitudes, and motivations it would be
best from the impersonal standpoint for them to have.[1] Thus, if
it can indeed be shown that an awareness of the strict proportionality requirement would undermine a person's integrity,
and if a person's integrity is a valuable thing, then we should not
expect any general consequentialist insistence that people be
aware of the strict proportionality requirement. And since a
belief in the correctness of consequentialism would presumably
lead people to an awareness of the strict proportionality
requirement, we should not even expect any general consequentialist insistence that people believe consequentialism to

[1] A consequentialist who took this claim seriously might as a result be led away from
standard act-consequentialism of the kind I am discussing, toward a view like the one
that Robert Adams calls 'act-and-motive utilitarianism' (see his 'Motive Utilitarianism', *Journal of Philosophy* 73 [1976]: 467–81). And having arrived at this sort of view,
such a consequentialist might then try to offer a different kind of argument in rebuttal of
the charge of insensitivity to integrity than the one I imagine in my text. I shall not
consider the merits of any such attempt, however, for it would not affect my main line of
argument. For further elaboration of this point, see footnote 26 of this chapter.

be correct. Quite to the contrary, we should expect widespread ignorance of the strict proportionality requirement and, more generally, of the correctness of consequentialism, to be required on consequentialist grounds. And we should expect consequentialism to require that people believe and be motivated by consequentialism only when, despite possible loss of integrity, these beliefs and motivations would be for the best overall and so serve to avert still more objectionable consequences. Thus, the defender of consequentialism may conclude, the charge that the theory systematically undermines the integrity of all agents is simply false. For the theory cannot undermine an individual's integrity if it does not require that the individual be aware of the strict proportionality requirement, and it requires such awareness only when this is necessary to promote the best outcomes. Thus at most consequentialism undermines the integrity of some agents. And these violations do not themselves constitute an objection to the theory in its more refined forms. For these versions of consequentialism will include integrity and related values among the goods which are somehow to be promoted, and so the violations of integrity which they require will characteristically serve the function of promoting states of affairs in which even greater numbers of people can lead integrated lives.[2]

There is ample precedent within the consequentialist tradition for the willingness, on which this defence depends, to enforce a radical separation between justification and motivation: between the moral requirements on action and the moral assessment of motives and beliefs. Sidgwick, for example, writes:

[T]he doctrine that Universal Happiness is the ultimate *standard* must not be understood to imply that Universal Benevolence is . . . always [the] best *motive* of action. For . . . it is not necessary that the end which gives the criterion of rightness should always be the end at which we consciously aim: and if experience shows that the general happiness will be more satisfactorily

---

[2] A consequentialist might use parallel lines of argument in an attempt to rebut other criticisms, such as the charge that consequentialism necessitates intolerable interpersonal manipulation and the charge that it leads to 'moral schizophrenia'. For versions of these criticisms, see, respectively, Adrian M. S. Piper, 'Utility, Publicity, and Manipulation', *Ethics* 88 (1978): 189–206, and Michael Stocker, 'The Schizophrenia of Modern Ethical Theories', *Journal of Philosophy* 73 (1976): 453–66.

attained if men frequently act from other motives than pure universal philan-
thropy, it is obvious that these other motives are reasonably to be preferred on
Utilitarian principles.[3]

Although consequentialists have found this line of thought
congenial, non-consequentialists characteristically argue that
there is something irrational or otherwise objectionable about a
principle of right action which, from its own point of view, may
not provide an acceptable source of motives or a permissible
basis for decision-making. Thus D. H. Hodgson writes:

the act-utilitarian principle is irrational: the whole point of the principle is
that the best possible consequences are to be promoted, and yet the adoption
of the principle would preclude the promotion of certain good consequences,
and would probably have worse consequences than acting upon more specific
rules. It is submitted that because of this irrationality, act-utilitarianism is not
a tenable ethical system.[4]

Although Hodgson's uneasiness is understandable, his
charge of irrationality does not seem persuasive as it stands. The
suggestion appears to be that utilitarianism thwarts its own
purpose and is thus self-defeating. But, in the first place, it is
not entirely clear what is meant here by the 'purpose' or 'point'
of utilitarianism, unless this is nothing more than a way of
referring to its content: utilitarianism (oversimplifying a bit) is
just the principle that the rightness of actions is a matter of their
producing the best possible consequences. And, in the second
place, there is no straightforward sense in which this principle
defeats its own 'point' so understood. For what is said by
Hodgson to be defeated is not the 'point' that the rightness of
actions is a matter of their producing the best consequences, but
rather the actual production of the best consequences. And
what is said by Hodgson to defeat this end is not the principle
itself, but rather its adoption by individuals as a guide or motive
of action. So the principle has not been shown to be self-defeating. Instead, what has been argued is that the end identified by
the principle as the criterion of right conduct would not be
furthered through its universal adoption as the conscious aim of

[3] *The Methods of Ethics*, p. 413.
[4] D. H. Hodgson, *Consequences of Utilitarianism* (Oxford University Press, 1967), p. 60.

human action.[5] And this does not show that the utilitarian principle is irrational, any more than the principle that students ought to stay calm during important examinations would be proven irrational if it should turn out that students who made calmness their conscious aim ended up tenser than they would otherwise have been.

It may be said at this point that even if utilitarianism is not irrational, any moral theory capable of requiring its own suppression surely violates one of the conditions of adequacy for such theories. Rawls, it may be noted, lists 'publicity' among the 'formal constraints of the concept of right';[6] the relative merits of different moral conceptions are to be assessed by imagining these conceptions as 'publicly acknowledged and fully effective moral constitutions of social life',[7] and then deciding which of the conceptions seems capable of playing this role most effectively. The publicity condition, as Rawls says,

> requires that in maximizing . . . utility we do so subject to the constraint that the utilitarian principle is publicly accepted and followed as the fundamental charter of society. What we cannot do is to raise . . . utility by encouraging men to adopt and apply non-utilitarian principles of justice. If, for whatever reasons, the public recognition of utilitarianism entails some loss of self-esteem, there is no way around this drawback. It is an unavoidable cost of the utilitarian scheme given our stipulations.[8]

In other words, the publicity condition has the effect of disallowing any defense of consequentialism which turns on the theory's willingness to require partial or complete ignorance of its own principles. The important questions for our purposes concern the origins and acceptability of the publicity condition itself.

Kurt Baier appears to believe that the condition of publicity or 'universal teachability'[9] is part of the concept or meaning of

---

[5] It should be noted that this argument, if correct, *would* suffice to show that utilitarianism is 'indirectly self-defeating', in Derek Parfit's special sense of that term. But, as Parfit agrees, even if utilitarianism is indirectly self-defeating in his sense, that does not cast doubt on the theory, let alone show that it is 'irrational' or 'untenable'. For Parfit's terminology, see his 'Is Common-sense Morality Self-defeating?', *Journal of Philosophy* 76 (1979): 533–45.

[6] *A Theory of Justice*, p. 130.

[7] Ibid., p. 133.

[8] Ibid., p. 181.

[9] Kurt Baier, *The Moral Point of View* (Cornell Univeristy Press, 1958), p. 196.

'morality'; he says that '"[e]soteric morality" is a contradiction in terms',[10] and that moral principles are 'meant to be taught to all members of the group in such a way that everyone can and ought always to act in accordance with these rules'.[11] Rawls himself is more circumspect. Although he counts publicity as one of 'the formal constraints of the concept of right', he does 'not claim that these conditions follow from the concept of right, much less from the meaning of morality'.[12] For, he says, '[t]he merit of any definition [of morality] depends on the soundness of the theory that results; by itself, a definition cannot settle any fundamental question'.[13] Thus the formal constraints of the concept of right are simply said to be 'conditions that it seems reasonable to impose'[14] on an adequate moral theory. Now I believe that Rawls is right to forgo any attempt to motivate the publicity condition through an appeal to the meaning of 'morality'. If 'morality' is defined in such a way as to include the publicity condition, and if a thoroughgoing consequentialism dispenses with the publicity condition, then talk about the relative merits of consequentialist and non-consequentialist moral principles can simply be recast as talk about the relative merits of consequentialist principles on the one hand and moral principles on the other. By itself, no simple appeal to meaning is capable of showing that there is something wrong with con-sequentialism's apparent willingness to violate the publicity condition. Although Rawls's attitude towards the publicity condition may thus be sounder than Baier's in the long run, it appears to provide no basis in the short run for a persuasive objection to consequentialist theories which violate that condi-tion. For once it is said that the condition is just something it 'seems reasonable' to expect an acceptable moral conception to satisfy, and that the adequacy of the condition must ultimately be assessed in light of the moral conception it leads to, the consequentialist can simply deny that the condition 'seems reasonable' to him, and force the discussion back to an overall

[10] Ibid., p. 196.
[11] Ibid., p. 195.
[12] *A Theory of Justice*, p. 130.
[13] Ibid., p. 130.
[14] Ibid., p. 130.

comparison of the consequentialist and non-consequentialist conceptions. And although Rawls's account manifests a conviction that a non-consequentialist moral conception which satisfies the publicity condition will, all things considered, seem more reasonable than a consequentialist conception which doesn't, his account does not seem to show that the violation of the publicity condition is, just in itself, unreasonable. It does not show that there is something wrong with the consequentialist attitude towards publicity *per se*.

By placing great weight on the distinction between justification and motivation, and by violating the publicity condition, the consequentialist can, as we have seen, construct a defence against the charge that his theory systematically undermines integrity. And so far, these moves have not been shown to render consequentialism irrational or unreasonable, or to disqualify it as a moral theory. To this point, then, we have been given no reason to reject the consequentialist reply to the objection dealing with integrity. Yet there is a persistent feeling of discomfort generated by the idea of a moral theory which is willing to require widespread ignorance of its own principles. Williams himself suggests that it is an idea that utilitarians and other consequentialists cannot embrace without forfeiting their only 'distinctive contribution':[15]

There is no distinctive place for . . . utilitarianism unless it is, within fairly narrow limits, a doctrine about how one should decide what to do. This is because its distinctive doctrine is about what acts are right, and, especially for utilitarians, the only distinctive interest or point of the question what acts are right, relates to the situation of deciding to do them.[16]

Thus, on Williams's view, utilitarians must pay a heavy price if they wish to make a sharp separation between justification and motivation, and to retain the ability to require non-utilitarian motives and beliefs.

If utilitarianism . . . determines nothing of how thought in the world is conducted, demanding merely that the way in which it is conducted must be

---

[15] Smart and Williams, *Utilitarianism For and Against*, p. 124. In the discussion of Williams that begins here, I take the liberty of construing his criticism as directed against act-consequentialism generally; he himself presents it only as a criticism of act-utilitarianism.

[16] Ibid., p. 128.

for the best, then I hold that utilitarianism has disappeared, and that the residual position is not worth calling utilitarianism.

If utility could be globally put together at all . . . then there might be maximal total utility from the transcendental standpoint, even though nobody in the world accepted utilitarianism at all. Moreover . . . it is reasonable to suppose that maximal total utility actually requires that few, if any, accept utilitarianism. If that is right, and utilitarianism has to vanish from making any distinctive mark in the world, being left only with the total assessment from the transcendental standpoint—then I leave it for discussion whether that shows that utilitarianism is unacceptable, or merely that no one ought to accept it.[17]

At the beginning of this chapter, I identified two options available to the consequentialist in constructing a reply to the charge that his theory systematically undermines personal integrity. One option was to deny the charge. The other was to concede its accuracy, but deny that it constitutes a weighty objection to consequentialism. Williams's remarks above may be construed as an attempt to disfigure these two options, recasting them in the form of an unwelcome dilemma for the consequentialist. If enough weight is placed on the distinction between justification and motivation to provide the basis for a rebuttal of the charge about integrity, then consequentialism itself vanishes, becomes empty, disappears. But if justification and motivation are not held radically separate, then the charge cannot be rebutted. So far in this chapter I have been discussing what I have called the consequentialist's 'first option', and I want to continue that discussion a bit longer, looking more closely at the first horn of Williams's dilemma. After that I will turn briefly to the second option, and the second horn of the dilemma.

Williams's idea is that since consequentialism's 'distinctive doctrine'[18] is its account of right action, and since, especially for consequentialists, the 'distinctive interest or point'[19] of an account of right action is to provide a basis for decision-making, it follows that if consequentialism deems its own principles generally unacceptable as a source of motives or a basis for decision-making, it gives up its only point, drains itself of any

[17] Ibid., p. 135.
[18] Ibid., p. 128.
[19] Ibid., p. 128.

interest, and effectively eliminates itself from serious consideration as a moral theory. If no one ought to accept the theory, then
what more is required to show it an unacceptable theory?

If the consequentialist chooses to seize this first horn of
Williams's dilemma, he may begin by simply denying one thing
that Williams asserts: that—especially for consequentialists—
the point of a conception of right action is to provide a basis for
decision-making.[20] No doubt there are philosophers who
regard that as the distinctive point of such a conception, the
consequentialist may say, but he of all people does not. He
views the point of a theory of right action as being to provide a
general account of what acts are right and what acts are wrong:
no more and no less. And for him the distinction between the
correctness or truth of any such theory, on the one hand, and
the advisability of widespread acceptance of the theory, on the
other hand, is a very important one. It is a distinction that he
emphasizes in connection with *all* theories, indeed all proposi-
tions, and not just in connection with moral theories. And, he
may rightly add, it is not only consequentialists who take the
distinction seriously in the case of *non-moral* theories. For
example, the seriousness of the distinction between truth and
advisability of acceptance is a presupposition of contemporary
debates, among parties not limited to consequentialists, about a
wide variety of topics: about whether to pursue nuclear
weapons research, or research which may increase our capacity
for genetic manipulation, to cite just two examples. To say that
the seriousness of the distinction is a presupposition of such
debates is obviously not to say that all of the participants in
these debates agree that there are some truths that ought to be
suppressed, or left undiscovered. It is simply to say that they
all recognize a serious and substantive difference between the
claim that something is true and the claim that it ought to be
generally believed; they do not regard the claim that a theory
ought not to be widely disseminated as equivalent or tantamount to the claim that the theory is false.

[20] My presentation of the consequentialist argument in this paragraph and the one
following has been heavily influenced by conversations with Peter Railton, and by his
unpublished paper 'Consequentialism and Integrity'. For a related discussion, see R.
Eugene Bales, 'Act-Utilitarianism: Account of Right-Making Characteristics or
Decision-Making Procedure?', *American Philosophical Quarterly* 8 (1971): 257–65.

What our consequentialist does is to take the distinction between truth and advisability of acceptance just as seriously in the case of moral principles. He refuses to regard the claim that a moral principle ought not to be widely believed as equivalent or tantamount to the claim that the principle is false or incorrect. And so when Williams suggests that it hardly matters whether one says that a moral principle is unacceptable or just that no one ought to accept it, the consequentialist who takes the line under discussion will regard this remark as a mere rhetorical flourish designed to trivialize a distinction that almost everyone takes seriously with regard to non-moral theories, and which this consequentialist sees every reason to take just as seriously in the moral case. It is perhaps worth mentioning that the idea that there are moral truths of which people ought not to be aware substantially predates the rise of modern consequentialism, it having notoriously found expression rather early on, in the form of a daunting but ultimately inefficacious prohibition against eating the fruit of one celebrated tree.[21]

There are two things worth mentioning about the line of argument just sketched in behalf of the consequentialist. The first point is that even consequentialists who profess to separate justification from motivation in the manner required by this argument do not always succeed in maintaining that separation consistently. Thus, for example, J. J. C. Smart, who explicitly follows Sidgwick in stressing the importance of the distinction between justification and motivation, also says that 'act-utilitarianism is meant to give a method of deciding what to do',[22] and that when a person 'has to think what to do, then there is a question of deliberation or choice, and it is precisely for such situations that the utilitarian criterion is intended'.[23] And this, as Williams notes, is just to say, inconsistently, that the utilitarian criterion is 'a matter of motivation, of what people should think about in deciding what to do'.[24] Now even if it is the case that consequentialists do not always find it easy to keep justi-

[21] See Genesis 2: 16–17.
[22] Smart and Williams, *Utilitarianism For and Against*, p. 44.
[23] Ibid., p. 43.
[24] Ibid., p. 125.

fication and motivation thoroughly separate, that in no way counts conclusively against the line of argument under consideration. But it does suggest that the publicity condition may be rooted in a view of morality whose appeal is not limited to anti-consequentialists, and whose influence on moral thought is considerable.

The second point, which is not unrelated, is that since the argument under discussion relies heavily on an analogy between scientific theories, truths, and knowledge, and between moral theories, truths, and knowledge, its persuasiveness will vary in accordance with varying attitudes towards that analogy. Clearly there are numerous meta-ethical standpoints from which the analogy will seem entirely inappropriate, and inappropriate for reasons which, if accepted, would serve to undermine the argument. Many people who do not consider themselves moral sceptics will feel that the content of practical principles is properly determined by their role in human social life in a way that the content of theoretical laws governing the behaviour of physical objects is not, and will moreover see the source of the publicity condition in this view of morality.

Although I am sympathetic toward this outlook, I do not in the end want to rest the case for an agent-centred prerogative on it. That is, I do not want to insist that consequentialism cannot legitimately violate the publicity condition,[25] or to conclude that since it does therefore systematically violate integrity, this constitutes a motivation for accepting an agent-centred prerogative. I prefer rather to leave open the question of the legitimacy of the violation of the publicity condition, and with it the question whether consequentialism really does systematically violate integrity. And I prefer instead to argue that even if the violation of the publicity condition *is* legitimate, and even if consequentialism does *not* violate personal integrity in a systematic way, there is still a motivation for favouring an ethical theory that includes an agent-centred prerogative.[26] In

[25] For an example of such insistence, see Philip E. Devine, 'The Conscious Acceptance of Guilt in the Necessary Murder', *Ethics* 89 (1979): 221–39.

[26] It should be remembered that in the text I am discussing only versions of standard act-consequentialism. Other forms of consquentialism, such as rule-consequentialism, or the 'act-and-motive utilitarianism' mentioned in footnote 1 of this chapter, might attempt to accommodate concerns about integrity without violating the publicity

other words, even if the objection dealing with integrity can be rebutted by the consequentialist, there is nevertheless a deep, principled rationale for the kind of device which enables the distributive hybrid to avoid that objection. If I am right about this, it may be taken as showing that even if the objection as it stands can be answered by the consequentialist, the intuitive uneasiness to which it gives voice can be seen to rest on a more defensible principled foundation.

This might appear to be a curious strategy for motivating an agent-centred prerogative, leaving unresolved as it does the question whether consequentialism undermines integrity. One might think that since such a prerogative is supposed to enable a theory to depart from consequentialism in such a way as to avoid undermining integrity, the availability of a motivation for it must depend wholly on the accuracy of the charge that consequentialism itself really does violate integrity. One might suppose, in other words, that if the charge were accurate, that would constitute a sufficient rationale for an agent-centred prerogative, and that if it were inaccurate, there would be no rationale for such a prerogative. But both parts of this supposition are mistaken. Suppose first that the charge were accurate. Before concluding that this constituted a genuine motivation for an agent-centred prerogative, it would still be necessary to come to grips with the second option available to the consequentialist in responding to that charge. Up until now, I have been focusing on ways in which the consequentialist might try to deny the accuracy of the charge. But it is, as I have noted, also open to him to seize the second horn of Williams's dilemma instead, by conceding that the charge is accurate, but denying that it constitutes a weighty objection to his theory, given the theory's various other advantages. Now in order to motivate an agent-centred prerogative in the face of this strand of consequentialist argument, one would have to give some account of the reasons for treating the violation of integrity as an over-

condition. For my purposes, however, there is no more need to assess the success or failure of such attempts than there is to finally determine whether standard act-consequentialism can rebut the objection dealing with integrity in the manner indicated in my text. For even if some or all of these forms of consequentialism can in the end avoid that objection, what I hope to show is that there is an independent rationale for an agent-centred prerogative.

riding defect in a moral theory. That is to say, one would have to provide an underlying rationale for such a prerogative, a rationale which went beyond the simple claim that a device of this kind enables a theory to accommodate considerations about personal integrity. So even if one were in the end to argue that consequentialism does systematically undermine integrity, it would still be necessary to provide a rationale at a deeper level for an agent-centred prerogative.

Suppose now that the charge about integrity were in-accurate. It would be wrong to conclude that there was no rationale for an agent-centred prerogative. For even if the charge as formulated missed its mark, it might still be that the underlying concerns which gave rise to the objection were both legitimate and capable of motivating such a prerogative. It may be noted, in this connection, that even if it were shown that consequentialism did not systematically undermine integrity, non-consequentialists would be likely to remain uneasy, feeling that this consequentialist sensitivity to integrity arose for the wrong reasons. While the non-consequentialist would of course need to show that this feeling was anchored in a serious under-lying motivation for rejecting consequentialism despite that theory's (supposed) sensitivity to integrity, the mere fact that such a feeling would exist rightly suggests that, whether or not the charge about integrity is accurate, the appeal of an agent-centred prerogative must depend on whatever underlying con-siderations can be advanced in its behalf. Now my strategy, as I have said, will be precisely to argue that whether or not con-sequentialism violates integrity, there exists a rationale of the appropriate kind for such a prerogative. So if the consequen-tialist takes his second option, conceding the accuracy of the charge about integrity but denying its importance, we can then respond by insisting that there *is* a serious motivation for a device which enables a theory to avoid the charge. On the other hand, even if the consequentialist takes his first option and succeeds in showing that his theory does not systematically undermine integrity, we can respond that there is nevertheless a plausible rationale for preferring a hybrid theory. Since I believe that it is possible to identify such a rationale, the case for an agent-centred prerogative does not in my view depend on the accuracy of the charge about integrity, and I do not mind leaving that as an unresolved issue. Even if one could finally show that the charge is accurate, this would in my view be an unnecessary shuffle, so far as attempts to motivate the prerogative go. For it would in any case still be necessary to provide the underlying rationale for such a prerogative, and this can be provided directly instead.

It may be wondered, however, why, if this is so, I have been discussing the objection from integrity at all. If the rationale for a prerogative is independent of the success or failure of the objection, why has so much time been spent examining the objection and possible replies? The answer is that whatever its ultimate merits *qua* criticism, the objection is one fairly intuitive expression of a certain kind of deep uneasiness which many people have felt about aspects of consequentialism. And by looking carefully at the objection, we can gain insight into the sources of that uneasiness. Of course, once we do succeed in achieving such insight, it is natural that we should begin turning our attention away from the initial objection and toward the sources of uneasiness themselves. For since our ultimate goal is to explore the most fundamental motivations for rival moral conceptions, we are less concerned with the accuracy of the charge about integrity *per se*, than with what this charge can teach us, one way or another, about the basic features of and rationales for such conceptions. And, as it turns out, we may learn most from the charge about integrity, in this regard, not by finally determining the accuracy of what it asserts, but by seeking out the sources of the dissatisfaction from which it springs. But this is quite evidently not to say that we might just as well have ignored the dispute about integrity altogether. There are many ways of learning from a criticism, not the least important of which is by coming to appreciate the implicit concerns that prompt it.

A programme for motivating an agent-centred prerogative having been outlined and defended in an abstract and schematic way, the time has now come to try to clothe this skeleton of a strategy in the flesh and blood of real diagnosis and understanding. It is time to make good the claim that whatever the merits of the objection from integrity *qua* criticism, consideration of the objection reveals a serious motivation for an agent-centred prerogative. I have said that the objection arises in response to the discrepancy between the way in which concerns and commitments are *naturally* generated from a person's point of view quite independently of the weight of those concerns in an impersonal ranking of overall states of affairs, and the way in which consequentialism requires the agent to treat the concerns generated from his point of view as altogether dependent for their *moral* significance on their weight in such a ranking. I have considered two ways a consequentialist might try to meet the objection: by denying that the discrepancy it responds to really has the effect of undermining personal integrity, or by conceding that it has this effect but denying the effect's importance. I want now to claim that whether or not the discrepancy has the effect of undermining integrity, there is a serious principled rationale for its elimination. How might this claim be defended? Here is one preliminary possibility.

It might be suggested that, in view of the discrepancy to which we have called attention, consequentialism ignores the independence of the personal point of view. This suggestion might be developed in the following way. Each person has a point of view, a perspective from which projects are undertaken, plans are developed, events are observed, and life is lived. Each point of view constitutes, among other things, a locus relative to which harms and benefits can be assessed, and *are* typically assessed by the person who has the point of view. This assessment is both different from and compatible with the assessment of overall states of affairs from an impersonal standpoint. That is just to say that some overall state of affairs that includes a given individual suffering may be the best available state of affairs impersonally judged, but at the same time its coming about may be a less than optimal outcome for this individual. The impersonal point of view, from which overall assessments of states of affairs are made, is only concerned with harms or benefits to any given individual in so far as those harms and benefits can be reckoned into the overall evaluation of the states of affairs they form parts of. From the impersonal standpoint, the fact that some person has a special kind of concern for his own projects and plans is relevant only in so far as it may affect the size of the harm or benefit incurred by that person when those projects fare poorly or well. Once that harm or benefit, however small or great, has been figured into the overall evaluation, the impersonal standpoint has no *further* concern with his projects. But *his* point of view is independent of the impersonal point of view, and this independence is typically evidenced by the fact that *he* cares differentially about his projects just because they are *his* projects. His interest in how they fare is not ordinarily exhausted by estimating the value or disvalue from the impersonal standpoint of their success or failure, and feeding this estimate into the impersonal calculus in order to arrive at an overall assessment *sub specie aeternitatis* of a contemplated outcome. His own projects and commitments have a distinctive claim on his attention; he cares about them out of proportion to the relative weight carried in the impersonal calculus by his having and caring about them.

Thus, the argument might continue, to have a personal point of view is to have a source for the generation and pursuit of personal commitments and concerns that is independent of the impersonal perspective. And, it might be said, consequentialism ignores this feature of persons. For it requires each person always to *act as if* he had no further concern for his projects and plans once the impersonal assessment was in. It singles out the impersonal calculus as identifying the right course of action for the individual, no matter how his own projects and plans may have fared at the hands of that calculus, and despite the fact that from the impersonal standpoint his own deepest concerns and commitments have no distinctive claim to attention. In other words, it requires that he devote energy to his projects in strict proportion to the weight from the impersonal standpoint of his doing so. And while this requirement may only undermine the individual's integrity if he is aware of it, and while it *may* be open to the consequentialist to mandate widespread ignorance of the requirement, it is in any event a decisive objection to consequentialism that it includes the requirement. For if, as Rawls has said, 'the correct regulative principle for anything depends on the nature of that thing',[27] we must surely

---

[27] *A Theory of Justice*, p. 29.

reject any regulative principle for persons which ignores the independence of the personal point of view. To have an independent point of view is part of the nature of a person if anything is. For the same reason, the argument might conclude, there is indeed a motivation for an agent-centred prerogative and for preferring hybrid to consequentialist theories, whether or not a prerogative is needed to prevent theories from undermining integrity. For by incorporating a plausible prerogative which allows agents to devote energy and attention to their projects and commitments *out of* proportion to the weight from the impersonal standpoint of their doing so, hybrid theories recognize and mirror the independence of the personal point of view.

This line of argument is overstated. Consider the response that might be made by a sophisticated consequentialist, who accepted a pluralistic account of the individual good like the one sketched in Chapter Two, and who used some distribution-sensitive principle for ranking overall states of affairs.[28] 'It is not true', such a consequentialist might begin, 'that our theory ignores the independence of the personal point of view, or that we are unaware of the special interest people typically take in their own projects and commitments. The difference between our theory and hybrid theories is not that they notice a morally important feature of persons which we overlook. It is rather that they think it is appropriate to take account of this feature in one way, and we think it is appropriate to do it another way. They believe that a moral conception should mirror the independence of the personal point of view. We do not. We believe that there is a way for a moral conception to give *more* weight to the admittedly important fact that each person has an independent standpoint and a special interest in his own projects and commitments: that is, by incorporating some distribution-sensitive principle for ranking overall states of affairs which reflects the desirability of as many people as possible pursuing their plans as successfully as possible, and then requiring each agent at all times to produce the best available state of affairs. Since this is

[28] Remember that I am imagining a sophisticated version of *act*-consequentialism. As I have repeatedly emphasized, it is only act-consequentialism that I am considering in this book.

just what our conception does, it ordinarily requires someone to abandon his projects only if that will serve to maximize the total number of people who can pursue their projects. And we recognize that it is almost always a hardship for a person to abandon his projects and commitments. So we always count the cost of such hardships in arriving at our overall assessments of relevant outcomes, thereby acknowledging the special concern people have for their projects *as their* projects. A person is ordinarily required to abandon his projects and commitments only if it turns out that, despite the hardship to him, it would maximize the total number of people able to carry out their projects and plans if he were to do this, thus producing the best available state of affairs impersonally judged. Of course, if it is ever psychologically *impossible* for an agent to abandon his projects, then of course we do not require it, for we require only that agents produce the best *available* states of affairs, and we do not regard a state of affairs as available to an agent if it would be impossible for him to produce it.

'Nevertheless, it has been alleged that, by requiring agents always to produce the best available states of affairs, our theory violates personal integrity. As we have seen, however, this allegation does not succeed if we are not prevented from separating justification and motivation. And even if it does succeed, we do not regard it as a very weighty objection, or one that undermines the rationality of our strategy for taking account of the independence of the personal point of view. Even if we do run afoul of the objection from integrity, we nevertheless take the independent individual with his distinctive concern for his projects and plans as seriously as it is possible to take him. For our idea, roughly, is that the number of individuals who successfully pursue their projects and plans should be maximized.[29] Any view which, like a hybrid conception, fails

[29] This formulation is only a rough one because there are two relevant variables: the number of people who successfully pursue their plans, and how successful each person is. Different consequentialist theories, by virtue of relying on different distribution-sensitive conceptions of the overall good, will balance these two considerations in different ways. But for the purposes of the 'sophisticated consequentialist' argument I am imagining, the rough formulation in the text, which leaves this matter open, is enough to make the intended point. For further discussion, see the penultimate paragraph of this chapter and footnote 35.

to require such maximization, thereby manifests a willingness to tolerate avoidable instances of numbers of people being unable to carry out their plans and satisfy their deepest aspirations. Thus any such conception actually gives less moral weight than we do to individual persons with their independent points of view and their diverse projects and commitments. Not only does our theory not ignore the independence of the personal point of view, it gives it more weight than a hybrid conception or any other conception does. Not only has it not been shown that there is a motivation for an agent-centred prerogative whether or not consequentialism violates integrity, the truth is rather that, either way, there is *no* defensible motivation for such a prerogative.'

This reply, like the argument *for* an agent-centred prerogative before it, is overstated. In order to settle the question about the rationale for such a prerogative, let me try to place both the argument and the reply in a more balanced perspective. It seems to me that there are different ways in which a moral conception can take account of the independence of the personal point of view. Sophisticated consequentialist conceptions do it one way, moral conceptions that incorporate an agent-centred prerogative do it another way. Neither type of view ignores this feature of persons. Sophisticated consequentialist conceptions take account of it by requiring, roughly, that each agent at all times act in a way that will serve to maximize the number of people who are successfully pursuing their projects and plans. I will call this 'the maximization strategy'. The guiding intuitions behind this strategy are two. The first is that if the independence of the personal point of view is an important fact for morality, that is because it fundamentally affects the character of human fulfilment and hence the constitution of the individual good. The second is that, given this conception of the importance of the fact of personal independence, a moral theory gives most weight to that fact if it seeks to maximize the number of individuals who actually achieve fulfilment from their points of view, by incorporating (a) some distribution-sensitive conception of the overall good which reflects the desirability of as many people as possible pursuing their plans as successfully as possible, and (b) a conception of the right which requires production of the best available states of affairs.

By incorporating an agent-centred prerogative, hybrid theories take account of the independence of the personal point of view in a different way. In order to appreciate the motivation for this alternative approach, let us reconsider some aspects of the maximization strategy. As we have seen, this strategy takes account of the person's nature as a being with a point of view by taking account from an impersonal standpoint of the significance to agents of personal commitments and projects, and of the hardships associated with abandoning such commitments and projects. If it turns out, despite the hardship to some given agent, that it would be best from the impersonal standpoint for him to abandon his projects, then he must do so, for the hardship to him has already been taken account of. Yet, as has been noted, having a personal point of view typically involves caring about one's projects and commitments out of proportion to their relative weight in the overall, impersonal sum. And so although the hardship to this agent may have been 'taken account of' from an impersonal standpoint, that is unlikely to exhaust his own feeling about the matter. But provided that this feeling has itself been assigned a 'cost' which has been fed into the impersonal calculus, it has no further moral relevance as far as the maximization strategy is concerned. This highlights a notable feature of the strategy: its insistence that the *moral* significance of a personal point of view, with its accompanying commitments and concerns, is entirely exhausted by the weight that point of view carries in the impersonal calculus, *even for the person who has the point of view*. Thus while sophisticated consequentialism does take account of the fact that persons have sources of energy and concern which are independent of the impersonal perspective, it does so in such a way as to deny that these points of view are *morally* independent. That is, it denies that personal projects and commitments can have any moral weight for an agent—any role in determining what the agent may do—independently of the weight those projects and commitments have in the impersonal calculus. Although sophisticated consequentialism takes account of the natural independence of the personal point of view, it, like other consequentialist theories, refuses to grant *moral* independence to this point of view.

A moral conception that incorporates an agent-centred prerogative, by contrast, takes account of the natural independence of the personal point of view precisely by granting it moral independence: by permitting agents to devote energy and attention to their projects and commitments out of proportion to the value from an impersonal standpoint of their doing so. I will call this 'the liberation strategy'. The guiding intuitions behind this strategy are two. The first is that if the independence of the personal point of view is an important fact for morality, that is not just because of its role in determining the nature of human fulfilment, but also, simply, because of what it tells us about the character of personal agency and motivation: people do not typically view the world from the impersonal perspective, nor do their actions typically flow from the kinds of concerns a being who actually did inhabit the impersonal standpoint might have. The second intuition is that, given *this* conception of the importance of the natural fact of personal independence, a moral view gives sufficient weight to that fact only if it *reflects* it, by freeing people from the demand that their actions and motives always be optimal from the impersonal perspective, and by allowing them to devote attention to their projects and concerns to a greater extent than impersonal optimality by itself would allow.[30]

Here, then, are two different ways in which moral theories can respond to the independence of the personal point of view. The two strategies appear to be incompatible: maximization precludes liberation, and liberation precludes maximization. Each strategy is said by its (imagined) adherents to give more weight than the other to the fact of independence. How can the conflict between these competing claims be resolved? Two possibilities suggest themselves.

First, of course, and most straightforwardly, one might try to resolve the conflict by showing that one of the claims is correct and the other incorrect: that one of the strategies simply does give more weight than the other to the independence of the

---

[30] The liberation strategy, incidentally, seems to me to capture most of what is worth capturing in Nozick's reminder that, with respect to each individual, 'his is the only life he has' (*Anarchy, State, and Utopia*, p. 33). Nozick himself believes that this reminder also points to a motivation for agent-centred restrictions. His argument seems to me unpersuasive, but I will not consider it until Chapter Four.

personal point of view. Thus, for example, someone might say: liberation really does give more weight to personal independence than does maximization, for the liberation strategy, by reflecting the natural independence of the personal point of view, gives weight to the fact of personal independence *per se*, while the maximization strategy, by seeking to increase fulfilment, only gives weight to the *effects* of independence.

The difficulties with arguments of this type are evident: to speak of a moral theory giving a certain amount of weight to some fact is to use a figure of speech, and one that is misleading to the extent that it suggests the possibility of precise measurement. It is simply not clear what standard one is supposed to use in comparing the 'weights' given to some fact by different moral conceptions. So it is not clear how one is to judge whether arguments of this type succeed or fail. Still, it may be possible to provide a clear standard for the relevant comparative judgements. But before deciding whether this is a task worth undertaking, let us consider the other possibility for resolving the conflict under discussion.

Rather than trying to show that one strategy really does give more weight than the other to the independence of the personal point of view, one might suggest that they are simply two different ways of giving weight to personal independence, with the choice between them properly dependent on one's ultimate moral attitudes, and not on any supposedly neutral determination of the magnitudes of the respective weights. The two strategies, as we have seen, are guided by different conceptions of the importance of personal independence. And each is a plausible strategy for acknowledging personal independence, in the following sense: each conceives of independence as an especially important fact under *some* (accurate) description, and embodies an evidently rational method for taking account of the fact so described. The maximization strategy regards independence as important primarily for the influence it exerts on the character of human fulfilment and hence the constitution of the individual good, and responds by seeking to maximize the number of individuals who succeed in achieving their good so understood. The liberation strategy, though compatible with a recognition of the effects of independence on the character of human fulfilment,[31] also emphasizes the importance of the natural independence of the personal point of view simply as a fact about human agency. It responds by insisting that the norms *governing* human agency must grant *moral* independence to every personal point of view, whatever account of personal fulfilment those norms rely on. Thus, one might suggest, the relative appeal of these two strategies will depend on one's ultimate moral attitudes, for there is no obvious or straight-forward sense in which the relative merits of the strategies are objectively decidable.

Which of these two ways of resolving the conflict seems the more promising? It is important to emphasize that my goal is to identify the principled rationale underlying an agent-centred prerogative, and so my interest in deciding which way to resolve the conflict is not intrinsic. I am concerned to make this deci-sion only if it is necessary to do so in order to reach that goal. Thus it is natural to begin by asking whether the two different methods for resolving the conflict would yield significantly different accounts of the rationale for the prerogative. Suppose, first, that one *could* show that the liberation strategy gives more weight than the maximization strategy to the independence of the personal point of view. Then one could say that whether or not consequentialism systematically undermines integrity, there is in any case a principled motivation for departing from consequentialism to the extent of accepting an agent-centred prerogative: namely, to give more weight than consquentialism does to the nature of a person as a being with a naturally independent point of view.

Now suppose instead that the liberation and maximization strategies were thought of as embodying two plausible ways of taking account of personal independence, with the choice between them a matter of one's ultimate moral attitudes. In this case, one could still say that there was a rationale for an agent-centred prerogative: namely, that it embodies a rational strategy for taking account of the nature of a person as a being with an independent point of view, given one construal of the importance of that aspect of persons. To be sure, the principled

---

[31] Recall that the distributive hybrid, for example, regards an individual's good as consisting in the pursuit of a rational plan of life.

motivation that would have been identified, given this second way of resolving the conflict, would not constitute a conclusive demonstration that moral conceptions that include an agent-centred prerogative are superior to consequentialist conceptions. Since the prerogative would have been motivated by showing that it gives rational expression to a certain ultimate moral attitude, it would appear to be legitimate for someone who lacked the attitude in question to reject the prerogative. Indeed, the sophisticated consequentialist might even propose as a rationale for *his* theory that *it* embodies a rational strategy for taking account of the nature of a person as a being with an independent point of view, given another construal of the importance of that aspect of persons. But remember that my project is not to give a conclusive proof of the superiority of hybrid conceptions, or to show that it is *only* hybrid conceptions whose salient structural feature has a plausible underlying motivation. The project is rather to conduct a comparative examination of two types of moral conceptions that depart from consequentialism: hybrid conceptions and fully agent-centred conceptions. In the case of hybrid conceptions, I am trying to show that not only is their salient structural feature responsive to certain intuitive objections to consequentialism, but that this feature also has an underlying principled rationale: it gives rational expression to some plausible attitude towards persons. Although I agree that agent-centred restrictions are similarly responsive to a variety of intuitive objections to consequentialism, I want to go on to explore the question whether there is a comparable underlying motivation for them. My project, in other words, is to explore the question whether agent-centred restrictions are as well-motivated as an agent-centred prerogative is. And for the purposes of this project, it appears that even if the conflict under consideration were resolved in the second way, a motivation of the requisite type for an agent-centred prerogative would still have been identified. For even given a resolution of this sort, it would have been demonstrated that such a prerogative does indeed embody a rational strategy for taking account of one significant feature of the person.

It may thus begin to seem that it is not essential to decide which way to resolve the conflict. For whether the liberation strategy gives more weight than the maximization strategy to the natural independence of the personal point of view, or whether instead the liberation strategy just constitutes one rational response to this aspect of persons, either way there appears to be a motivation for an agent-centred prerogative of just the right sort.

Someone might suppose, however, that the rationale for a prerogative would be much stronger if one could resolve the conflict in the first way, showing that the liberation strategy really does give more weight to personal independence than the maximization strategy. Then, it might be thought, we really would have a conclusive demonstration that hybrid theories are superior to consequentialist theories. But it would be a mistake to think this. Even if 'sophisticated consequentialists' were forced to agree that they had been wrong in claiming that their theory gives more weight than hybrid theories to personal independence, it is not at all obvious that they would then have to concede the inferiority of their theory. They might instead reason as follows: 'It has already been agreed that the maximization strategy embodies an evidently rational procedure for acknowledging personal independence, given our construal of the importance of that feature of persons. Now, even if it can be said that this strategy gives less weight to independence than the liberation strategy does, in some absolute sense, that does not show that the maximization strategy is *not* a rational method for acknowledging independence, after all. For it does not show either that our construal of the importance of independence is untenable, or that the relation between that construal and the maximization strategy is any less close than it initially appeared to be. What it does show instead is that, given our interpretation of the importance of independence, a strategy that gives it less weight is the strategy it is rational to prefer.' The apparent availability to the sophisticated consequentialist of this response confirms the suspicion that it is not necessary to decide how to resolve the dispute under consideration. No matter which way the dispute is resolved, there is in any case a rationale for an agent-centred prerogative of just the right sort. And no matter which way the dispute is resolved, the identification of the rationale does not constitute a conclusive demonstration of the absolute superiority of hybrid theories or the absolute inferiority of consequentialist theories.

It is thus possible, at long last, to state the rationale for an agent-centred prerogative in its final form. Whether or not there is some absolute sense in which hybrid theories incorporating an agent-centred prerogative give more weight than consequentialist theories to the natural independence of the personal point of view, the prerogative is, at the very least, a structural feature whose incorporation into a moral conception embodies a rational strategy for taking account of personal independence, given one construal of the importance of that aspect of persons.

In leaving open the question of absolute weight, I am continuing to follow a policy of not attempting to resolve any question whose resolution is not actually a precondition of accomplishing the goals of the project I have undertaken. The motivation for this policy is to avoid weighing the project down with extraneous and controversial 'meta-ethical' commitments which could artificially limit its interest and appeal. Other applications of the policy in this section have resulted in the setting aside of arguments against consequentialism which appeal to the meaning of 'morality', on the one hand, and to apparent disanalogies between ethics and science, on the other hand. And the fact that it has proved possible to identify a rationale for an agent-centred prerogative has not been presented as an indication that hybrid theories are objectively correct, though the possibility that they are objectively correct has not been ruled out either; no position at all has been taken on the question of whether it is appropriate to seek an objectively correct moral theory.

This is not to say that my project has no presuppositions that may be thought of as meta-ethical. Although the distinction between meta-ethics and normative ethics is itself problematic, to say the least, there seems no point in denying that my discussion of the comparative rationales for different moral doctrines presupposes a willingness, which may not be shared by everyone, to think about those doctrines in a certain light. I have already made it clear, first, that I consider it appropriate to seek comprehensible and rationally defensible explanations of the salient structural features of different moral theories, and second, that I am willing to count it as an explanation of the relevant kind that a particular feature may be thought of as representing a demonstrably rational response to a certain feature of persons. These are my two most important presuppositions, and there are doubtless people who would reject them. The first might perhaps seem misguided to some who regard moral judgements as nothing more than expressions of approval and disapproval, for it might seem to them to carry with it an inappropriate expectation about the extent to which the set of any given person's moral views may plausibly be thought of as having an even putatively rational structure. The second might seem wrong-headed to some who regard moral theory as analogous to (or a branch of) scientific theory, for it might seem to them inappropriately tolerant of the idea that the content of an acceptable moral theory may be determined by possibly variable conceptions of or attitudes toward the person. And there may of course be other and better examples of people who would reject the presuppositions of the project I have undertaken, and regard the project itself as idle or misconceived.

This having been said, however, it in no way undermines my claim to have avoided taking meta-ethical stands that are unnecessary for the purposes of the project, nor does it defeat the goal of that abstention. The point to bear in mind is that although the project most certainly requires a willingness to regard moral conceptions in a certain light, its meta-ethical presuppositions nevertheless remain relatively minimal. In particular, the project does not presuppose the correctness of some particular, fully developed meta-ethical view, where such a view is understood to include an account of such issues as the subjectivity or objectivity of morality, how a moral view is ultimately to be justified, and the nature of moral motivation. All that is necessary for someone to find the project of value is that he think it an interesting question whether different moral structures can be seen to have underlying rationales of a comprehensible sort, and that he have no rigid and unusual prejudices about what sorts of rationales are to count as comprehensible. It seems to me overwhelmingly likely that proponents of a number of different meta-ethical views will fit this description. My project may perhaps be genuinely incompatible with some meta-ethical views, and on the other hand it may seem a particularly natural and congenial undertaking from certain[32] other perspectives. But by striving to avoid resolving questions whose resolution is not actually required for the completion of my project, and by thus seeking to emphasize that the project's meta-ethical presuppositions are relatively minimal, I hope to show that its interest is not restricted to proponents of a particular meta-ethical view, and may in fact be quite broad.

Before concluding this section, let me return to an issue I alluded to at the outset. In investigating the rationale for an agent-centred prerogative, I have been assuming that the prerogative has some form that makes it responsive to the objection dealing with integrity, but I have not been assuming that it must have the particular form sketched in Chapter Two. And it appears that very different versions of the prerogative may be equally responsive to the objection dealing with integrity. To take an extreme case, an egoist version of the prerogative, according to which each agent was *always* permitted to pursue his own projects and advance his own interests, whatever they were, might well be responsive to concerns about integrity. Since the discussion of the motivation for an agent-centred prerogative has not presupposed a *particular* form of the prerogative, it seems that the choice among forms as radically divergent as the one sketched in Chapter Two and the egoist version just mentioned may be underdetermined by the motivational considerations I have identified. In order to adequately motivate the particular version of the prerogative presented in Chapter Two, an underlying principled rationale would have to be identified for the restrictions that that version places on the legitimate pursuit of personal projects and plans. Nothing that has yet been said would persuade an egoist that restrictions of this sort are appropriate.

[32] I have sketched one such view in 'Moral Scepticism and Ideals of the Person', *The Monist* 62 (1979): 288–303, 'Ethics, Personal Identity, and Ideals of the Person', *Canadian Journal of Philosophy* 12 (1982): 229–43, and 'Reply to Darwall', *Canadian Journal of Philosophy* 12 (1982): 257–62. Another such view is developed by Rawls in his Dewey Lectures, *Journal of Philosophy* 77 (1980): 515–72.

Now to be sure, any non-egoistic moral conception must ultimately come to grips with the egoist challenge. But it is not part of my project to undertake that task. As I have said repeatedly, I am engaged in a comparative examination of the motivations underlying two types of non-consequentialist moral devices: the agent-centred prerogative and agent-centred restrictions. As part of this investigation, I have shown that there is an underlying principled rationale for an agent-centred prerogative, and also that such a prerogative *need not* take an egoist form; it can take a form like the one suggested in Chapter Two. But it is not part of this investigation to address the question of why, ultimately, such a prerogative *ought not* to take an egoist form. Important as it is, the question what is wrong with egoism is beyond the scope of my undertaking.

II

Just as my discussion of the rationale for an agent-centred prerogative began with a reconsideration of the objection dealing with integrity, so too my discussion of the rationale for a distribution-sensitive conception of the overall good will begin with a reconsideration of the objection dealing with distributive justice. However, this second discussion will be much shorter than the first. There are three reasons for this. The first is that the issues surrounding the topic of distributive justice have been more thoroughly discussed in the contemporary literature than have the issues relating to personal integrity. The second reason is that there are some significant parallels between the debate about integrity and the debate about distributive justice; having discussed the former thoroughly, it may be possible to treat the latter more expeditiously. The third reason is this. While the objection dealing with integrity, which prompted the introduction of an agent-centred prerogative, arises in response to the conception of the right that all consequentialist theories share, the objection dealing with distributive justice, which prompted the introduction of a distribution-sensitive principle for ranking overall outcomes, arises ultimately in response to a particular conception of the overall good which only utilitarianism among consequentialist theories includes. And while an agent-centred prerogative is a defining feature of all hybrid theories and is incompatible with all consequentialist theories, a distribution-sensitive ranking principle is not a necessary feature of either hybrid or consequentialist theories, although such a principle *can* be included within either type of framework. Thus although the presentation of the rationale for such a principle is a necessary part of the process of motivating distribution-sensitive hybrid conceptions, such as the distributive hybrid outlined in Chapter Two, it is not a part of the process of motivating hybrid conceptions as a class. And although I hope to show that the motivation for a certain kind of distribution-sensitive principle is closely connected to the motivation for an agent-centred prerogative, nevertheless a dispute about the strength of the motivation for such a principle should have no direct bearing on one's judgement about the merits of hybrid theories generally. It should not directly affect one's judgement about the relative plausibility of the three main types of moral conceptions that I am discussing: consequentialist, hybrid, and fully agent-centred conceptions.

In discussing the rationale for an agent-centred prerogative, I supposed only that the prerogative had some form which made it responsive to the objection dealing with integrity; I did not assume that it had the particular form suggested in Chapter Two. Now in discussing the rationale for a distribution-sensitive principle for ranking overall states of affairs, I will be assuming that such a principle relies on a pluralistic account of an individual's good like the one described in Chapter Two, and that the principle takes some form that makes it responsive to the objection dealing with distributive justice. But I will not be supposing that it must take the particular form of 'the distributive principle' sketched in Chapter Two. Although, as I have indicated, I believe that the distributive principle is the most plausible version of a distribution-sensitive ranking principle, the choice between that version and others which are also capable of accommodating concerns about distributive justice, and which also rely on the pluralistic account of an individual's good, may be underdetermined by the motivational considerations I shall identify. Thus some people who find those con-

siderations compelling may nevertheless prefer some distribution-sensitive ranking principle other than the distributive
principle.

With this in mind, let me now turn to the reconsideration of
the objection dealing with distributive justice. Classical utilitarianism, as we've seen, includes a conception of the overall
good that ranks states of affairs from best to worst according to
the amount of total satisfaction they contain. Given any two
overall states of affairs, classical utilitarianism will rank the one
with greater total satisfaction higher, no matter how wide a
range there may be in the levels of well-being of different people
within the state of affairs with the higher total. When combined
with a conception of the right that always requires the production of the best states of affairs, this conception of the overall
good exposes the resulting utilitarian theory to the charge that
it will frequently require us to ignore the misery of a few and
concentrate instead on increasing the pleasures of the many,
simply in order that total aggregate satisfaction may be maximized. Now there are, as I've said, some significant parallels
between the debate about integrity and the debate about distributive justice. The consequentialist, as we saw earlier, may
respond to the charge that his theory systematically undermines personal integrity either by denying the accuracy of the
charge or by conceding its accuracy but denying its importance.
Similarly, the utilitarian may either deny the charge that his
theory will frequently require us to ignore the misery of a few
and concentrate instead on increasing the pleasures of the many
simply in order that total aggregate utility may be maximized,
or he may concede the accuracy of the charge but deny that it is
a serious objection to his view.

Utilitarians who deny the charge typically argue that
although their view is committed in principle to the idea that
some people's life prospects should be sacrificed in order to
increase the non-essential satisfactions of others whenever that
will maximize total aggregate utility, such sacrifices rarely do
maximize total utility in practice. In practice, they argue, the
best available state of affairs, the one containing the highest
level of aggregate utility, will almost never be one in which some
people are miserable and many others are extravagantly well

off. Thus substantially inegalitarian policies almost never maximize overall utility, and, as it happens, the pursuit of more or less egalitarian goals constitutes an effective strategy for maximizing total satisfaction. At their crudest, such suggestions can appear to be no more than *ad hoc* attempts to mitigate unattractive but genuine consequences of the theory. But many people feel that, by invoking plausible empirical assumptions about the diminishing marginal utility of money and related phenomena, defenders of utilitarianism can make a stong case for the view that a society governed by their principles would be a considerably egalitarian society. And if this view is indeed correct, defenders of utilitarianism are sure to add, there can be no objection to the occasional large inequalities that the theory may in fact require. For just like the more egalitarian norm itself, they will say, these occasional large inequalities are embraced because they serve the single overriding purpose of maximizing total satisfaction.

The empirical assumptions relied on in this strand of utilitarian argument are not entirely uncontroversial. But even if these assumptions are sound, and even if it is thus correct to claim that utilitarianism will rarely require that we ignore the misery of a few people and concentrate instead on increasing the pleasures of the many simply in order that total satisfaction may be maximized, non-utilitarians are likely to remain uneasy, just as non-consequentialists would remain uneasy even if it could be shown that consequentialism does not systematically undermine integrity. For the utilitarian still maintains that the best available state of affairs is always the one in which total satisfaction is maximized, no matter how benefits and burdens are distributed within the state of affairs. So he still believes that the life prospects of a few should be sacrificed in order to increase the non-essential satisfactions of the many whenever that will maximize total satisfaction. He simply doubts that this will as a matter of fact be the case very often. And non-utilitarians are bound to feel that this still leaves the legitimacy or illegitimacy of such sacrifices dependent on a mistaken conception of the best overall states of affairs. Some non-utilitarians may actually feel that a state of affairs in which the life prospects of a few are neglected while non-essential interests of the better off are satisfied can *never* be better than an alternative state of affairs in which the life prospects of those few are preserved and the non-essential interests of the better off left unsatisfied. Other non-utilitarians may feel that a state of affairs of the first type can *sometimes* be better than one of the second type: if, for example, it would for some reason be unusually difficult or costly to preserve the life prospects of a few people, and the result would be a marked decrease in the quality of life for a sizeable number of other people. But these non-utilitarians are all likely to agree that considerations about how benefits and burdens are distributed among different people have an importance which does not depend exclusively (if at all) on any role distribution may play in maximizing total satisfaction, and that therefore the mere fact that a state of affairs of the first type has a higher level of aggregate satisfaction than a state of affairs of the second type is not by itself sufficient, even in principle, to show that the first state of affairs is better than the second. They are likely to agree, in other words, that there is an independent principled rationale for admitting distributive considerations directly into the evaluation of overall states of affairs.

Since I myself share this view, I do not want to rest the case for a distribution-sensitive conception of the overall good on the claim that utilitarianism frequently requires us to ignore the misery of a few and concentrate instead on increasing the advantages of the many simply in order that maximum total satisfaction may be achieved. Just as there are significant parallels between the debate about distributive justice and the debate about integrity, so too the strategy for motivating a distribution-sensitive ranking principle will be parallel to the strategy for motivating an agent-centred prerogative. I will leave open the question of how often utilitarianism would actually require that some people's life prospects be sacrificed simply in order that total satisfaction might be maximized, just as the question whether consequentialism systematically undermines integrity was left open. And I will argue instead that even if utilitarianism does *not* require this very often, there is nevertheless a serious underlying rationale for a distribution-sensitive ranking principle, just as I argued earlier that there is a motivation for an agent-centred prerogative whether or not consequentialism systematically undermines integrity. If my argument is successful, then it will not matter which option the utilitarian takes in responding to the objection dealing with distributive justice. Whether he denies the charge that his theory will frequently require us to ignore the misery of a few and concentrate instead on increasing the pleasures of the many simply in order that total utility may be maximized, or whether he concedes the accuracy of the charge but denies that it is a serious objection to his view, either way we will be able to respond that there is in any case a plausible rationale for incorporating a distribution-sensitive ranking principle into a hybrid or consequentialist conception. Thus what I hope to show is that even if the objection based on distributive justice can be rebutted by the utilitarian, there is nevertheless an underlying principled rationale for the kind of device whose incorporation into the distributive hybrid was designed to enable it to meet that objection. If I am right about this, it may, as I suggested earlier, be taken to show that even if the objection as it stands can be answered by the utilitarian, the intuitive uneasiness to which it gives voice can be seen to rest on a more defensible principled foundation.

It is important to repeat that the issue at hand is not one that divides consequentialist theories, as a class, and hybrid theories, as a class. The choice under consideration is between a traditional utilitarian principle for ranking overall states of affairs and a distribution-sensitive principle. Each type of principle is capable of being incorporated into either a consequentialist or a hybrid conception. I am attempting to provide a rationale for a certain kind of distribution-sensitive principle, and if I succeed that rationale will be available to defenders of consequentialism as well as to defenders of hybrid conceptions. The choice between these two kinds of theories themselves must be made on other grounds; my own position on that question should of course be clear from my earlier discussion of the motivation for an agent-centred prerogative. What I now wish to show is that whether or not utilitarianism frequently requires us to ignore the misery of a few and concentrate instead on increasing the pleasures of the many simply in order to maxi-

mize total satisfaction, there exists a rationale for a certain type
of ranking principle which can clearly enable either a hybrid
conception or a consequentialist conception to avoid requiring
this.

What, then, is the rationale for a distribution-sensitive conception of the overall good? To be accurate, I will really be
addressing a narrower question here. For, as I have already
indicated, although I will not be assuming in my discussion that
such a conception must take the specific form of 'the distributive principle' sketched in Chapter Two, I will be assuming
that it relies on a pluralistic account of an individual's good like
the one relied on by the distributive principle. And although
that account of the individual good is not uncontroversial, I will
not attempt to defend it here.[33] Instead, the question I will be
addressing is this: what is the rationale for a distribution-
sensitive principle for ranking overall states of affairs, *given* the
pluralistic account of an individual's good?

It is true that this leaves it open to hedonistic and preference-
satisfaction utilitarians to maintain that, given their rival
accounts of the individual good, a principle for ranking states of
affairs that incorporates a simple maximizing structure will
seem better motivated than a principle that is distribution-
sensitive. There are two points to be emphasized in response.
The first is that these claims may or may not be true. Although
the rationale for a distribution-sensitive principle, as I shall
present it, assumes a certain view of the individual good, it may
turn out that this rationale seems persuasive even when one
substitutes alternative views of individual good. I suspect that
this is in fact the case though I will not try to defend that
suggestion. The second point is that, as with the project of
motivating an agent-centred prerogative, it is important not to
lose sight of the goals of the enterprise. In both cases, my stated
aim has been to identify a plausible principled motivation
underlying the preference for a moral view incorporating the
structural feature in question. In neither case have I claimed

---

[33] As we saw in our discussion of the agent-centred prerogative in the first section,
however, the independence of the personal point of view may itself be thought to affect
the constitution of the individual good in such a way as to make an account of personal
good like the one relied on by the distributive principle seem plausible.

that no rival view could be found for which it would similarly be possible to identify a principled underlying rationale. Thus, in the case at hand, the fact that a possible avenue for motivating utilitarian accounts of the overall good is being left open in no way undermines my project. What I hope to show is that, given one standard and widely shared conception of the *individual* good, it is possible to identify a plausible principled rationale for an *overall* ranking principle that incorporates a distribution-sensitive structure.

The motivation for a distribution-sensitive ranking principle, like the motivation for an agent-centred prerogative, is connected with the nature of the personal point of view. A distribution-sensitive principle represents a rational way for a ranking principle to take account of the distinctness of persons, given a certain conception of persons and of their good.[34] As I have said, each person has a point of view, a perspective from which projects are undertaken, plans are developed, and life is lived. And the good for a person, as I conceive it, consists in successfully carrying out a rational plan of life. Different persons, each one with his own projects and plans, are distinct, though to say this is obviously not to deny the reality or importance of empathy, identification, sharing, co-operation, joint activity, and other related aspects of human experience. Indeed, as a moment's thought will show, these phenomena all presuppose the distinctness of persons.

Now competing principles for ranking overall states of affairs involve competing claims about what it is best to have happen in the world. The various pluralistic, distribution-sensitive principles that are responsive to the objection dealing with distributive justice represent different ways of giving clear content to the intuitive idea that the best state of affairs is one in which as many distinct people as possible are carrying out their

[34] For some doubts about the moral importance of the separateness of persons, see Derek Parfit, 'Later Selves and Moral Principles' in *Philosophy and Personal Relations*, Alan Montefiore, ed. (London: Routledge & Kegan Paul, 1973): 137–69. See also Parfit's earlier paper, 'Personal Identity', *Philosophical Review* 80 (1971): 3–27, and his later paper, 'Lewis, Perry, and What Matters', in *The Identities of Persons*, Amelie Rorty, ed. (Berkeley: University of California Press, 1976): 91–107. The last of these is a response to papers by David Lewis ('Survival and Identity') and John Perry ('The Importance of Being Identical'), both of which are also contained in Rorty's anthology (pp. 17–40 and 67–90, respectively).

plans as successfully as possible, and are hence achieving their good. This intuitive idea needs to be supplied with clear content for two reasons. First, some criterion is needed for assessing and comparing the extent to which different people are succeeding in carrying out their plans. Offhand, this kind of success does not appear to be something which readily lends itself to precise assessment or interpersonal comparison, especially in view of the irreducibly heterogeneous nature of personal plans. The ranking principles I am discussing solve this problem by treating a hierarchy of levels of well-being as equivalent to a hierarchy of degrees of success, and by using a standard that is 'objective', in the sense described in Chapter Two, as a measure of well-being. Second, the intuitive idea by itself is indeterminate, in that it identifies two things that are to be maximized: the number of people who successfully carry out their plans, and the degree of success each achieves. And it does not specify how these two considerations are to be balanced in concrete situations. Is it better that ninety-nine people should be very successful in pursuing their plans and one only somewhat successful, or that all hundred should be moderately successful? Different pluralistic, distribution-sensitive principles will, in effect, answer questions such as these in different ways. This particular question, for example, might be answered one way by a lexical ranking principle or an egalitarian principle, and another way by the distributive principle. Thus different principles of this kind represent different ways of resolving the indeterminacy of the intuitive idea that what is best to have happen is that as many people as possible should be carrying out their plans as successfully as possible. For they represent different ways of balancing the two maximands contained in that intuitive formula. These various pluralistic, distribution-sensitive principles may therefore be thought of as embodying different versions of a maximization strategy for ranking overall states of affairs.[35] But in keeping with the idea that persons are

[35] What is the relation between the different versions of this maximization strategy for responding, in the ranking of overall states of affairs, to the distinctness of persons, and the maximization strategy employed by 'sophisticated consequentialism' as a means of responding to the independence of the personal point of view? Recall that the latter strategy involves incorporating (a) some distribution-sensitive conception of the overall good which reflects the desirability of as many people as possible pursuing their

distinct and that the good of each consists in striving to carry out his projects and plans, the maximization in question is not maximization of 'the good', conceived as an additive psychological quantity or as utility, but rather of the number of people who are successfully carrying out their plans, and of the degree of success each is achieving.

In view of these remarks, we may say that whether or not utilitarianism would regularly require the sacrifice of some people's life prospects simply in order that total aggregate satisfaction might be maximized, there is in any case a principled motivation for a distribution-sensitive principle which clearly enables a moral conception to avoid doing this. While the agent-centred prerogative embodies a rational strategy for taking account in a conception of the right of the fact that persons are *naturally independent of the impersonal standpoint*, given one interpretation of the importance of such independence; a distribution-sensitive ranking principle embodies a rational strategy for taking account in a conception of the overall good of the fact that persons are *naturally distinct from each other*, given one conception of persons and of their individual good.[36]

plans as successfully as possible, and (b) a conception of the right which requires production of the best available states of affairs. Thus the maximization strategy for responding to the independence of the personal point of view *presupposes* some version of a maximization strategy for ranking overall states of affairs, but it goes further in requiring that individuals always produce the best state of affairs so characterized. For a related discussion, see Chapter Five, p. 124.

[36] The idea that a *lexical* ranking principle represents one rational response to the distinctness of persons is in certain obvious respects reminiscent of Rawls's view. But Rawls does not appear to recognize that a form of consequentialism could incorporate such a principle and so take account of the separateness of persons. There is no argument given against pluralistic lexical consequentialism in *A Theory of Justice*.

4

THE DEFENCE OF AGENT-CENTRED RESTRICTIONS: INTUITIONS IN SEARCH OF A FOUNDATION

AGENT-CENTRED restrictions, I have said, are restrictions on action which have the effect of denying that there is any non-agent-relative principle for ranking overall states of affairs such that it is always permissible to produce the best available state of affairs so construed. I want now to characterize these restrictions more fully, and to explain why they have this effect. An agent-centred restriction is a restriction which it is at least sometimes impermissible to violate in circumstances where a violation would prevent either more numerous violations, of no less weight from an impersonal point of view, of the very same restriction, or other events at least as objectionable, and would have no other morally relevant consequences. Imagine a theory according to which there is some restriction S, such that it is at least sometimes impermissible to violate S in circumstances where doing so would prevent a still greater number of equally weighty violations of S, and would have no other morally relevant consequences. Now S is an agent-centred restriction; due to the inclusion of S in the theory, there exists no non-agent-relative principle for ranking overall states of affairs from best to worst such that it will always be permissible to produce the best state of affairs so characterized. If the best overall state of affairs is construed as the one containing fewest violations of S, for example, it will at least sometimes be impermissible for an agent to produce that state of affairs if he can only do so by actually committing one of the (minimized) violations of S. Thus agent-centred restrictions are limitations on the conduct of the individual agent which take priority over calculations of overall impersonal value.

An agent-centred prerogative, as we have seen, serves to deny that agents are always *required* to produce the best overall states of affairs. Agent-centred restrictions, on the other hand, serve to deny that there is any non-agent-relative principle for ranking states of affairs such that agents are always *permitted* to produce the best state of affairs. Both devices thus represent departures from consequentialism, which takes the impersonal standpoint to be the only moral standpoint. Intuitively, it may therefore seem plausible that the rejection of agent-centred restrictions should be ultimately imcompatible with acceptance of an agent-centred prerogative. For it may seem that if there is a motivation for introducing any agent-centredness into a moral theory at all, then there is a motivation for introducing *both* agent-centred components. And if the introduction of one agent-centred component is poorly motivated, then the introduction of the other component must be poorly motivated as well. Hence it may appear that there are only two positions one can consistently hold: one can either reject agent-centredness altogether and retreat to some kind of consequentialism, or accept a fully agent-centred view incorporating both an agent-centred prerogative and agent-centred restrictions. Hybrid conceptions, it may seem, represent an attempt to stake out a middle ground that does not exist; there is no room for a view intermediate between consequentialist and fully agent-centred conceptions. There is no room for a conception that incorporates an agent-centred prerogative but not agent-centred restrictions.

I believe that this intuitive line of reasoning is mistaken, and that hybrid views constitute a bona fide alternative to consequentialist and fully agent-centred conceptions. I believe that there is an underlying principled motivation for an agent-centred prerogative, and that this motivation has been identified in the last chapter. And I believe that this motivation is independent of any rationale there may be for agent-centred restrictions, in the sense that someone who is motivated in this way to accept a prerogative can at the same time consistently refuse to accept such restrictions. I will call this *the independence thesis*. The truth of the independence thesis is of course compatible with the existence of some separate principled motivation for agent-centred restrictions. Not only do I believe that the independence thesis is true, however, I also believe, as I have indicated, that it is surprisingly difficult to find plausible suggestions in the literature as to what an underlying motivation for such restrictions might be. There is thus another thesis that in my opinion merits our close attention. *The asymmetry thesis* asserts that although it is possible to identify an underlying principled rationale for an agent-centred prerogative, it is not possible to identify any comparable rationale for agent-centred restrictions. If the independence thesis alone were true, then hybrid theories would still represent a bona fide alternative to consequentialist and fully agent-centred conceptions. But if the asymmetry thesis were also true, then fully agent-centred conceptions might begin to look particularly problematic. In this chapter, I want to examine possible rationales for agent-centred restrictions. In the course of the discussion, I will defend the independence thesis, and try to explain why the asymmetry thesis must also be taken seriously.

As I suggested in Chapter One, there are some prima-facie difficulties with agent-centred restrictions. The main problem is the apparent air of irrationality surrounding the claim that some acts are so objectionable that one ought not to perform them even if this means that more equally weighty acts of the very same kind or other comparably objectionable events will ensue, and even if there are no other morally relevant consequences to be considered. An adequate principled motivation for agent-centred restrictions must dispel this air of irrationality. It must provide answers to a series of questions posed by Nozick:

Isn't it *irrational* to accept a side constraint C, rather than a view that directs minimizing the violations of C? . . . If nonviolation of C is so important, shouldn't that be the goal? How can a concern for the nonviolation of C lead to the refusal to violate C even when this would prevent other more extensive violations of C? What is the rationale for placing the nonviolation of rights as a side constraint upon action instead of including it solely as a goal of one's actions?[1]

[1] *Anarchy, State, and Utopia*, p. 30. 'Side constraint' is Nozick's term for the kind of agent-centred restriction he favours.

As I begin to explore possible answers to these questions, I want to re-emphasize at the outset that, despite the apparent air of irrationality to which I have called attention, the intuitive appeal of agent-centred restrictions is not in question. Such restrictions are certainly responsive to widely shared anti-consequentialist sentiments. There are many imaginable cases, for example, in which many people would intuitively feel it wrong to kill an innocent person even if doing so would prevent two or three other equally objectionable killings, and would have no other morally relevant consequences. It is to feelings of this sort that agent-centred restrictions respond, or appear to respond. Thus the intuitive appeal of such restrictions is not in question, just as the intuitive appeal of an agent-centred pre-rogative was never in question.

However, while the fact that a structural feature has intuitive appeal constitutes a reason for trying to identify a plausible rationale for that feature, it does not constitute a rationale of the sort I am looking for, nor guarantee that there is one. In now familiar fashion, a consequentialist might respond in either of two ways to the charge that his theory regularly generates results which violate the intuitions to which agent-centred restrictions answer. He could respond either by denying that such cases arise often in real life and claiming that occasionally counter-intuitive positions may nevertheless be acceptable, or by conceding that such cases arise regularly but denying the importance of the counter-intuitive character of the con-sequentialist position, especially in light of the prima-facie irrationality of the more intuitive fully agent-centred concep-tions. So what we wish to know is whether it is possible to establish that whether or not consequentialism regularly yields counter-intuitive consequences in real-life cases, there is in any event a principled rationale for agent-centred restrictions. If this could be established, then if the consequentialist took his second option, conceding that his theory yields systematically counter-intuitive results but denying the importance of that point, the defender of agent-centred restrictions could respond by insisting that there *is* a serious underlying motivation for the restrictions which respond to those anti-consequentialist intuitions. And even if the consequentialist took his first option and succeeded in showing that his theory does not regularly yield counter-intuitive results in real cases, the defender of the restrictions could respond that there is nevertheless a plausible rationale for preferring a fully agent-centred conception. With the restrictions as with the agent-centred prerogative, then, the existence of supporting intuitions marks the beginning and not the end of the search for an underlying principled rationale.

To focus the discussion of possible rationales for agent-centred restrictions, let us consider a schematic example of a disagreement between those who accept such restrictions and those who reject them. Suppose that if agent A_1 fails to violate a restriction R by harming some undeserving person P_1, then five other agents, $A_2 \ldots A_6$, will each violate restriction R by identically harming five other persons, $P_2 \ldots P_6$, who are just as undeserving as P_1, and whom it would be just as undesirable from an impersonal standpoint to have harmed. We may make the following simplifying assumptions: (1) A_1 has no way out of this dilemma, and (2) there are no morally relevant consequences of A_1's action or non-action beyond those already mentioned. Neither these simplifying assumptions nor the case as I have described it manifests any bias against agent-centred restrictions. Consider the simplifying assumptions first. Obviously, in real-life cases there are likely to be more options available to the agent, some important long-term consequences to take into account, and greater uncertainty about the outcomes of the various actions. But the assumptions that exclude these complications serve only to guarantee that we have a clear example of the kind of case that gives rise to disagreement between those who accept agent-centred restrictions and those who reject them; the simplifications in themselves count neither for nor against such restrictions.

Consider now the description of the case itself. Different fully agent-centred conceptions differ with regard to what exactly they take the agent-centred restrictions on action to be, and so they would differ about which specific restriction should play the role of restriction R. Just for this reason, the content of R was left deliberately vague in describing the case; no unusual or prejudicial assumptions were made about the character of the restriction.[2] Similarly, there is wide variation among fully agent-centred conceptions with regard to the circumstances, if any, under which the restrictions are thought to be overridable. At one end of the spectrum, 'absolutist' conceptions hold that some restrictions cannot be overridden and must not be violated, whatever the consequences. Some non-absolutists occupy an intermediate position, conceding only that agent-centred restrictions *sometimes* give way: when we are threatened

[2] There is, however, an important qualification that must be made at this point. It is true that I am taking R to be a restriction against nothing more specific than 'harming some undeserving person'. And it is true that every fully agent-centred view which has any degree of plausibility does include restrictions which answer to that description. But it is also true that most such conceptions also take there to be other sorts of agent-centred restrictions as well. Thus, according to most such conceptions, we are at least sometimes obligated to keep our promises even if we could produce a better overall outcome by not doing so. And it is also typically held that we have special obligations to protect and promote the interests of people to whom we stand in certain special relations, to our parents, children, spouses, patients, students, and so on, and that these obligations may not be violated whenever a violation would lead to a better overall outcome. Agent-centred restrictions of these two kinds are not most accurately described simply as restrictions against harming.

As I have argued, a hybrid conception, unlike a consequentialist conception, would ordinarily *permit* agents to keep their promises, or to promote the interests of people to whom they stand in special relations, even if by not doing so they could produce better overall outcomes. For a hybrid conception permits people to devote energy and attention to their projects, commitments, and personal relationships out of proportion to the weight from an impersonal standpoint of their doing so. And, as I have also argued, a hybrid conception might additionally require agents to keep their promises and fulfil their voluntarily incurred special obligations *unless* their not doing so would result in a better overall outcome. But fully agent-centred conceptions obviously go further, maintaining that there are times when promises must be kept and obligations fulfilled *even if* failure to do so would result in a better overall outcome.

Now in my discussion of possible rationales for agent-centred restrictions, I will, as I have said, be treating a restriction R against harming some undeserving person as my paradigm case of such restrictions. But although some of the arguments I will offer will be in criticism of supposed rationales for agent-centred restrictions like R in particular, I will also offer a number of arguments in criticism of supposed rationales for agent-centred restrictions in general, and, as a result, a number of perfectly general arguments about the form that a rationale for *any* kind of agent-centred restriction must take. It is true, however, that I will not directly discuss any specific proposals that might be made for motivating *only* those agent-centred restrictions which prohibit the breaking of one's promises or the neglect of one's special obligations. And, strictly speaking, this leaves it open to a defender of a fully agent-centred outlook to maintain that those restrictions have a rationale of the appropriate form which is independent of any putative rationale for restrictions like R, and which remains compelling even if doubt is cast on the strength of supposed general rationales for agent-centred restrictions, and on the strength of specific rationales for agent-centred restrictions against harming in particular.

by an evil that is so great as to seem immeasurable, and honouring *them* means losing everything. Toward the other end of the spectrum, finally, there are those non-absolutists who go much further, holding that it is often (though not always) permissible to violate the restrictions in circumstances where doing so is the only way to prevent a still greater number of equally weighty violations of the very same restrictions, or other events at least as objectionable. One might caricature these differing positions by saying that the absolutist would prohibit the violation of a restriction even if a violation were the only way to prevent a genocidal catastrophe,[3] the more restrictive non-absolutist would permit a violation in circumstances such as these but not in situations any less catastrophic, and the less restrictive non-absolutist would permit one violation if that would prevent twenty comparable violations but not if it would prevent only three. Although the absolutist variant may place the greatest strain on the credibility of fully agent-centred conceptions, the case I have described does not respond to distinctive features of absolutist conceptions, and hence in using this example I am not attempting to exploit specially problematic aspects of such conceptions. In other words, the example does not prejudice the issue by depicting catastrophic consequences if A_1 fails to violate R and then assuming that defenders of agent-centred restrictions as a class are committed to forbidding violation. The outcome of non-violation is not extreme, relatively speaking, and the case could easily be redescribed in such a way as to make the outcome still less extreme, without changing the

[3] Consider Ivan Karamazov's challenge to his brother Alyosha in Dostoevsky's novel:

> Tell me yourself, I challenge you—answer. Imagine that you are creating a fabric of human destiny with the object of making men happy in the end, giving them peace and rest at last. Imagine that you are doing this but that it is essential and inevitable to torture to death only one tiny creature—that child beating its breast with its fist, for instance—in order to found that edifice on its unavenged tears. Would you consent to be the architect on those conditions? Tell me. Tell the truth.

(*The Brothers Karamazov* (New York: New American Library, 1957), p. 226.)

Ivan's question does not constitute a sufficient test for absolutism. In order to be an absolutist, it is not enough to hold that it would be impermissible to torture one child to death even if that would produce universal happiness. One must also hold that it would be impermissible to torture one child to death even if that were the only way to prevent, say, everyone else in the world's being tortured to death.

basic issues. For if the non-absolutist is committed to agent-centred restrictions at all, then there must be some restriction R, such that in some situation, he will say that an agent is required not to violate R even though a still greater number of equally weighty violations of R, or other comparably objectionable events, will ensue if the agent does not violate R, and even if there are no other morally relevant consequences to be considered. And it is claims of this type about cases of this sort, made by absolutists and non-absolutists alike, which I wish to explore. The example sketched is intended as a schematic idealization of one such case: no more and no less.

Let me then adapt Nozick's question to my example: why isn't the view that it is wrong for A_1 to violate R irrational?[4] There is one way of trying to answer the question which may seem tempting initially, but which is also clearly unacceptable. That is, it is tempting to suggest that acts that violate R have some feature that is very bad or has high disvalue, and that it is for this reason that A_1 may not violate R. But this suggestion is clearly inadequate, for, *ex hypothesi*, however high the disvalue of a violation of R, a greater number of equally weighty violations—and hence at least as much disvalue—will ensue if A_1 does *not* violate R. Appeals to the disvalue of violations of R are powerless to explain why it is wrong to violate R when doing so will prevent five identical violations of R.[5]

Nevertheless, defences of agent-centred restrictions in the literature often seem to take the form of an appeal to the

[4] There is one kind of possible answer to this question that I will not even consider: the kind of answer that might be given by defenders of rule-consequentialism, act-and-motive consequentialism, or other such views. For an elaboration of this point, see footnote 7 of this chapter.

[5] Compare T. Nagel:

> . . . the constraints on action represented by rights cannot be equivalent to an assignment of large disvalue to their violation, for that would make it permissible to violate such a right if by doing so one could prevent more numerous or more serious violations of the same right by others. This is not in general true. It is not permissible . . . to kill an innocent person even to prevent the deliberate killing of three other innocent persons. A general feature of anything worthy of being called a right is that it is not translatable into a mere assignment of disvalue to its violation.

('Libertarianism Without Foundations', *Yale Law Review* 85 (1975), at p. 144.)

disvalue of violation. Thus, for example, Nozick, answering his own question about the apparent irrationality of 'side constraints', says: 'Side constraints upon action reflect the underlying Kantian principle that individuals are ends and not merely means; they may not be sacrificed or used for the achieving of other ends without their consent. Individuals are inviolable.'[6] It is natural to interpret this passage as a suggestion that violations of agent-centred restrictions involve violating the victimized individuals themselves, treating them as means instead of ends, and that since being violated or treated as a means is a bad thing, violations of such restrictions are impermissible. It is natural, in other words, to interpret Nozick's defence of side constraints as an appeal to the disvalue of certain features of violations of the constraints. But if this *is* the proper interpretation of his defence, then clearly that defence is inadequate for the reasons just mentioned.

The general point, which applies to agent-centred restrictions of all kinds, may be illuminated by looking at this particular defence, as applied to our schematic example, more closely. Presumably, persons $P_1 \ldots P_6$ in our example are all equally 'inviolable', in the sense that Nozick intends. Yet, *ex hypothesi, someone* in that example is going to be violated. Either A_1 will harm P_1 or five other agents will identically harm $P_2 \ldots P_6$. Either way, someone loses: *some* inviolable person is violated. Why isn't it at least permissible to prevent the violation of five people by violating one? An appeal to the value of an unviolated life or the disvalue of the violation of a life cannot possibly provide a satisfactory answer to this question. For the question is not whether to choose an unviolated life over a violated one; the relative value of violated and unviolated lives is not at issue. Instead, the choice is between one person inflicting a relatively smaller number of violations, and five other persons inflicting a relatively larger number of violations of equal weight from an impersonal standpoint. And the question is what possible ground there is for holding that the one person must not inflict the smaller number of violations in order to prevent their more numerous occurrence. The badness of a

[6] *Anarchy, State, and Utopia*, pp. 30–1.

violation cannot provide such a ground, for surely five violations are at least as bad as one.

Similarly, the badness of being treated as a means to some end cannot account for the impermissibility of A_1's violating R by harming P_1 in order to prevent five other agents from identically harming $P_2 \ldots P_6$. For once again, *ex hypothesi, someone* will be treated as a means to an end whatever A_1 does. If it is indeed a bad thing to be treated as a means to an end, why isn't it at least permissible for A_1 to treat one person as a means to some end if that will prevent five other equally undeserving people from being so treated? At least the person A_1 uses will be treated as a means to the end of minimizing the treatment of people as means. Even if we leave this last point aside, however, the badness of being treated as a means to an end cannot provide a ground for the impermissibility of A_1's treating P_1 as a means to an end in this case. For surely five such treatments of no less weight from an impersonal standpoint are at least as bad as one.

As we have seen, the problem is with the general strategy for the defence of agent-centred restrictions that is employed here. So long as the strategy is to single out some feature of violations of the restrictions as having high disvalue, no adequate defence of such restrictions will emerge. It makes no difference, in particular, *which* feature of violation is singled out as having a high disvalue: no difference, for example, whether the focus is on the victim of violation, the agent, or the relationship between them. One might address the defender of agent-centred restrictions as follows. If, in our example, you are concerned about the badness of what will happen to P_1 if A_1 violates R (P_1 will be used, treated as a means, or whatever), why isn't it permissible to be at least as concerned about the fivefold badness of what will happen to $P_2 \ldots P_6$ if A_1 does *not* violate R (then they will be used, treated as means, etc.)? If instead you are concerned about the badness of a human agent *doing* something harmful to another human being, why isn't it permissible to be at least as concerned about the badness of *five* human beings doing equally harmful things to five other human beings. And if you are worried that a violation of R corrupts the *relationship* between the agent and the victim, and that the corruption of a human relationship is a bad thing, then why isn't it at least permissible to corrupt one valuable relationship if that is the only way to prevent the corruption of five equally valuable human relationships?

An attempt to motivate agent-centred restrictions by appealing to the disvalue of violations of such restrictions is directly analogous to an attempt to motivate an agent-centred prerogative by appealing to the value or goodness of an agent's carrying out his projects and plans. Both attempts fail, for parallel reasons. An appeal to the disvalue of violations of a restriction is powerless to explain why one may not violate that restriction in order to prevent still more numerous violations, of no less weight from an impersonal standpoint, of the very same restriction. Thus such an appeal cannot motivate agent-centred restrictions. It can only motivate a consequentialist presumption against performing the kinds of acts that such restrictions forbid, a presumption that is overridable whenever the disvalue of a violation would be exceeded by the disvalue of the consequences of non-violation. Similarly, an appeal to the value of an individual's carrying out his plans is powerless to explain why one is not required to abandon one's *own* plans if doing so would enable still more people to carry out *their* plans. Such an appeal cannot therefore motivate an agent-centred prerogative. All it can do is to motivate a provisional consequentialist dispensation to devote more attention to one's own happiness and well-being than to the happiness and well-being of other people so long as doing so will have the best results overall. In sum, appeals to value cannot succeed in motivating either of the agent-centred structural components we are examining. They cannot provide a rationale either for agent-centred restrictions or for an agent-centred prerogative. They can only serve to motivate consequentialist presumptions and consequentialist dispensations: those strategic manoeuvres internal to consequentialism which constitute that conception's alternative to, and substitute for, the radical departures of agent-centred morality.[7]

[7] Remember that, in speaking of consequentialist presumptions and dispensations, I am referring to the strategic manoeuvres available to the standard act-consequentialist. As I noted in footnote 4 of Chapter Two, defenders of other forms of consequentialism might argue in favour of some other kind of dispensation which represented a departure from strict act-consequentialism. Now it is also true that some rule-con-

Clearly, the failure of attempts to motivate agent-centred restrictions by appealing to the disvalue of violations of such restrictions does not indicate that no plausible rationale whatsoever can be found for such restrictions, any more than the failure of attempts to motivate the agent-centred prerogative by appealing to the value of individual plans indicates that there is no plausible rationale for that device. The lesson to be learned from the failure of the parallel appeals to value is rather that any successful attempt to motivate either agent-centred component will have to take a different form. Although an agent-centred prerogative cannot be motivated through an appeal to value, I have of course already argued that it is possible to motivate such a prerogative by showing how it embodies a rational strategy for taking account of the independence of the personal point of view, given one construal of the importance of that aspect of persons. The question now to be faced is the question of whether, similarly, it is possible to identify a plausible underlying rationale for agent-centred restrictions, even though *they* cannot be motivated through an appeal to value.

The first possibility to consider, along these lines, is the possibility that someone who embraces the motivation for an agent-centred prerogative is thereby committed, on pain of inconsistency, to accepting agent-centred restrictions as well. The suggestion here, in other words, is that the independence thesis is false. This suggestion has a certain amount of initial implausibility. For, as we have seen, the prerogative and the

---

sequentialists, or act-and-motive consequentialists, might try to defend something stronger than an act-consequentialist presumption against performing the acts which agent-centred restrictions forbid. Some might go so far as to say that, depending on how our schematic example was filled out, with regard to such things as the motives of $A_2 \ldots A_6$, it might indeed be wrong for A_1 to violate R. Others who insisted that it would be right for A_1 to violate R might nevertheless add that there are good, broadly consequentialist reasons for agents not to be disposed to do the right thing in such cases. As I have repeatedly emphasized, I am limiting my discussion of consequentialism in this book to act-consequentialism, so I will not attempt to assess the merits of any broadly consequentialist arguments for the view that A_1 ought not to violate R, or that A_1 ought to be disposed not to violate R even if violating R is what he really ought to do. What I am trying to determine is whether or not traditional deontological views are correct to maintain, as I believe they do maintain, that just as there is a rationale for an agent-centred prerogative which is independent of even broadly consequentialist considerations, so too there is a rationale for agent-centred restrictions which is independent of even broadly consequentialist considerations.

restrictions respond to different sorts of anti-consequentialist intuitions. This is not conclusive, however, for intuitions with differing content may nevertheless have sources which are closely linked, or even a single source in common. So despite its initial implausibility, the suggestion that the independence thesis is false needs to be taken seriously. As I have character-ized it, the motivation for an agent-centred prerogative is that it embodies a rational strategy for responding to the natural independence of the personal point of view, given a certain legitimate construal of the importance of independence. Now this implies that one is not rationally required to go beyond that strategy and accept agent-centred restrictions additionally in response to the fact of independence so conceived. Thus, assuming that my characterization of the motivation for an agent-centred prerogative is accurate, it seems quite likely that the independence thesis is true, and the suggestion we are considering false. It is not yet certain, however. For even if someone who accepts the prerogative as embodying a rational response to the independence of the personal point of view, given a certain construal of the importance of independence, is not thereby committed to accepting agent-centred restrictions additionally in response to the fact of independence so con-strued, there remains the possibility that such a person *is* also thereby committed to some separate strategy for responding to something *other* than the fact of independence so construed, and that this second strategy *does* constitute a motivation for agent-centred restrictions. But although this is an abstract possibility, I cannot think of any way to make it concretely plausible. There is nothing that emerged in the course of the discussion of the liberation strategy that provides any reason for thinking that the employment of this strategy commits one to using other sorts of strategies in other sorts of circumstances. I conclude that this abstract possibility may be discounted, and that there-fore the independence thesis is true, and the suggestion we have been considering is false. It is not the case that someone who embraces the motivation for an agent-centred prerogative is thereby committed, on pain of inconsistency, to accepting agent-centred restrictions as well. It is not the case that one must either reject agent-centredness altogether and retreat to consequentialism, or accept a fully agent-centred view which incorporates both an agent-centred prerogative and agent-centred restrictions. Hybrid theories constitute a bona fide, stable alternative to consequentialist and fully agent-centred conceptions.

It is important to note that the independence thesis is nevertheless compatible with the possibility that fully agent-centred conceptions embody *some* rational strategy for responding to the independence of the personal point of view. For all that has been said so far, it may be that fully agent-centred conceptions and hybrid conceptions employ two equally rational strategies for responding to the fact of personal independence, given two equally legitimate construals of the importance of that fact, or even given the very same construal of its importance. It may be that the choice between these strategies depends on one's ultimate moral attitudes. All that has been ruled out is the possibility that everyone who accepts an agent-centred prerogative as part of a response to personal independence must also accept agent-centred restrictions. The possibility that hybrid conceptions and fully agent-centred conceptions represent *alternative* responses to the fact of independence remains open, and it is natural to examine this possibility next.

Do agent-centred restrictions embody all or part of a rational strategy for responding to the natural independence of the personal point of view, given some legitimate construal of the importance of that aspect of persons? There is an initial implausibility about the suggestion that they do, just as there was an initial implausibility about the suggestion that the independence thesis is false. The implausibility of both proposals derives from the fact that they both take the underlying motivations for the two agent-centred devices to be closely connected, even though those devices respond on the surface to very different kinds of anti-consequentialist intuitions. As I noted in connection with the previous proposal, however, surface differences can conceal underlying connections. So the current proposal, like the previous one, must be taken seriously.

It seems to me that the most plausible way of developing the proposal is by trying to understand agent-centred restrictions as representing all or part of a rational response to the independence of the personal point of view, given an interpretation of the importance of that aspect of persons which is just the same as the interpretation relied on by the liberation strategy. For the current proposal is like the liberation strategy in seeking to construe an agent-centred feature of moral theories as a rational response to the independence of the personal point of view. It is thus most plausible to suppose that, if agent-centred restrictions do represent a rational response to personal independence, they, like the agent-centred prerogative, do so given a conception of the importance of independence which emphasizes its significance for human agency. Since this is the most plausible way of developing the current proposal, I will make it the focus for my consideration of the proposal as a whole. If the proposal in its strongest form is ultimately defective, it is reasonable to pass over alternative construals that had less promise from the start.

Thus the question is whether it is in fact appropriate to conceive of agent-centred restrictions as constituting all or part of a rational response to the natural independence of the personal point of view, given that the importance of independence is conceived as stemming primarily from its impact on the character of human agency and motivation. I believe that the answer to this question is 'no'. Someone who disagreed might reason thus. Agent-centred restrictions, which have the effect of denying that there is any non-agent-relative principle for ranking overall states of affairs from best to worst such that it is always permissible to produce the best available state of affairs so characterized, serve to protect individuals from the demand that they organize their conduct in accordance with some canon of impersonal optimality. They prevent individuals from becoming slaves of the impersonal standpoint, and in so doing they serve to insulate the personal point of view against external demands. For this reason they represent a rational response to the fact that individuals are naturally independent of the impersonal perspective.

As it stands, this line of argument is inadequate. The *permission* not to produce the best states of affairs suffices to free individual agents from the demands of impersonal optimality, and thus to prevent them from becoming slaves of the impersonal standpoint. That is the whole point of the liberation strategy, which underlies the agent-centred prerogative. What must be provided is a rationale for going beyond such permissions and *prohibiting* the production of the best states of affairs. Of course, since prohibitions against producing the best states of affairs entail permissions not to produce those states of affairs, it is true that agent-centred restrictions do free agents from the requirement always to do what would have the best outcome overall.[8] But this does not show that such restrictions are, after all, a rational response to the natural independence of the personal point of view, for the fact that a prohibition entails a motivated permission does not constitute a motivation for the prohibition.

Someone might try in the following way to improve on the argument I have just rejected. It is true, it might be conceded, that an agent-centred prerogative suffices to free individuals from the requirement always to do what would have the best outcome overall. But it is not true that prohibitions against doing what would have the best outcome accomplish nothing further, in this regard. By always permitting actions that would have the best outcome overall, hybrid conceptions leave open the possibility of morally acceptable conduct which is guided exclusively by the standard of impersonal optimality. Fully agent-centred conceptions, by contrast, eliminate this option. They insist that the acceptability of an individual's conduct must be determined by the intrinsic characteristics of his personal projects, actions, and intentions, and not by an extrinsic, impersonal appraisal of those overall states of affairs which his actions may produce. In this way, fully agent-centred conceptions grant more extensive moral independence to the personal point of view that hybrid conceptions do. For while

[8] This passage calls to mind a kind of moral conception of which I have not yet taken note. The non-consequentialist conceptions I have been discussing depart from consequentialism either by incorporating an agent-centred prerogative alone, or an agent-centred prerogative *and* agent-centred restrictions. Non-consequentialist conceptions of the second type, which I have been calling 'fully-agent centred' conceptions, include two kinds of permissions not to produce the best states of affairs: those conferred by the prerogative and those entailed by the restrictions. As this passage suggests, however, one can imagine moral conceptions that did include agent-centred restrictions but that did not include any permissions not to produce the best states of affairs *except* those entailed by the restrictions.

hybrid conceptions regard it as morally tolerable if an individual always does what will have the best overall outcome
impersonally judged, fully agent-centred conceptions insist
that the standards of individual conduct must be specially
tailored to fit the *personal* perspective of the individual agent.
Thus, the argument might be summed up, fully agent-centred
conceptions do embody a rational response to the natural independence of the personal point of view, given one legitimate
construal of the importance of independence. Like hybrid conceptions, they regard independence as important primarily for
its impact on the character of human agency. Unlike hybrid
conceptions, however, they respond by insisting that human
agents must be held to a standard of accountability which gives
the intrinsic qualities of an individual's acts moral priority over
their impersonal optimality.

This revised argument seems to me to represent the strongest
kind of case that can be made for construing agent-centred
restrictions as part of a rational response to the independence of
the personal point of view, but I believe that it is flawed none
the less. The intuitive idea behind the argument is that a moral
conception gives priority to the personal point of view over the
impersonal point of view, and thus emphasizes the independence of the former from the latter, by insisting that individuals
be judged on the basis of the intrinsic qualities of their personal
actions, projects, and intentions, and not on the basis of an
impersonal appraisal of the tendency of their conduct to promote the overall good. However, in so far as the argument does
suggest a principled motivation for departing from consequentialism, the motivation suggested is for an agent-centred prerogative only. And in so far as the argument purports to provide
a motivation for agent-centred restrictions, it fails to do so.

The basic problem is that the argument misconceives the
nature of the individual point of view. It implicitly assumes that
an individual cannot, from his own point of view, form and act
on intentions to do things that will have the best overall outcome, either because they will have the best outcome, or for
other reasons. Individuals cannot identify with acts and intentions of this kind. Activities that promote the best overall states
of affairs cannot be among a person's projects. If the argument

were not relying on these assumptions, there would be no plausibility whatsoever to its claim that fully agent-centred conceptions give the personal point of view priority over the impersonal point of view by holding the individual to a standard of accountability which gives the intrinsic personal qualities of his actions and projects priority over their impersonal optimality. For if actions which will have the best overall outcome *can* be undertaken from within the individual's own point of view, then the agent-centred restrictions which limit such actions, far from representing a way of giving the personal point of view priority over the impersonal point of view, will appear instead as arbitrary and unexplained constraints on the projects and activities of the individual.

The assumptions that the argument thus relies on are evidently false. A person may want to do what will have the best overall outcome, either because it will have the best outcome or for some other reason. Thus A_1, in our schematic example, might decide to violate R because he genuinely wanted to do what would have the best overall outcome, and believed that violating R would, or because he had compassion for all six potential victims and wanted to prevent as many of them as possible from suffering. One can also intend to do and *actually* do that which will have the best outcome, either because it will have that outcome or for other reasons. Moreover, one can identify with these wants, intentions, and actions in just the same way that one identifies with others of one's wants, intentions and actions. They are just as compatible with the personal point of view as, for example, desires, intentions, and actions to promote the good of particular people one cares about. The promotion of the general good, like the promotion of the good of one's intimates, can be undertaken from *within* one's personal standpoint. This is unproblematic. Since the assumptions relied on by the argument are thus false, the argument fails to support agent-centred restrictions. For, as I have already noted, once it is recognized that actions and projects that promote optimal outcomes can be undertaken from within one's personal point of view, then the agent-centred restrictions which limit such actions no longer appear to be a way of giving the personal point of view priority over the impersonal point of view, but look instead like arbitrary and unmotivated constraints on the projects and activities of the individual. Hybrid conceptions, by contrast, do not impose restrictions of this kind on personal projects. And, of course, they give the agent permission to devote energy and attention to his projects, plans, and personal relationships out of proportion to the weight in the impersonal calculus of his doing so. Thus they, more than fully agent-centred conceptions, may be thought of as specially tailoring the standards of individual conduct to fit the personal perspective of the individual agent, and in this way of giving moral priority to the personal point of view. That is what I meant when I said earlier that, in so far as the argument I have been considering does suggest a principled motivation for departing from consequentialism, the motivation suggested is for an agent-centred prerogative only, and in so far as the argument purports to provide a motivation for agent-centred restrictions, it fails to do so. It seems fair to conclude that, even in its most plausible form, the idea of construing agent-centred restrictions as part of a rational response to the independence of the personal point of view is unacceptable.[9] Let us thus turn our attention to other suggestions for motivating such restrictions.

If agent-centred restrictions cannot be construed as part of a rational response to the natural independence of the personal point of view, can they instead be seen as part of a rational strategy for responding to some other feature of the person? We may consider, in this connection, another suggestion of Nozick's, which is reminiscent of the proposals of his that we have already considered, though somewhat different:

. . . why may not one violate persons for the greater social good? Individually, we each sometimes choose to undergo some pain or sacrifice for a greater benefit or to avoid a greater harm: we go to the dentist to avoid worse suffering later; we do some unpleasant work for its results; some persons diet to improve their health or looks; some save money to support themselves when they are

[9] The argument of the last three paragraphs has been intended in a very general way as a response to the account given by Thomas Nagel, in his Tanner Lectures, of the foundations of deontological moral conceptions. Those lectures have been published, with the overall title 'The Limits of Objectivity', in *The Tanner Lectures on Human Values I*, Sterling McMurrin, ed. (University of Utah Press and Cambridge University Press, 1980): 77–139. See especially pp. 126–39.

older. In each case, some cost is borne for the sake of the greater overall good. Why not, *similarly*, hold that some persons have to bear some costs that benefit other persons more, for the sake of the overall social good? But there is no *social entity* with a good that undergoes some sacrifice for its own good. There are only individual people, different individual people, with their own individual lives. Using one of these people for the benefit of others, uses him and benefits the others. Nothing more. What happens is that something is done to him for the sake of others. Talk of an overall social good covers this up. (Intentionally?) To use a person in this way does not sufficiently respect and take account of the fact that he is a separate person, that his is the only life he has. *He* does not get some overbalancing good from his sacrifice, and no one is entitled to force this upon him . . .[10]

If this passage is interpreted as appealing, in defence of agent-centred restrictions like R, to the disvalue of some features of violations of such restrictions—the feature of disrupting the only life the victim has, for example—then it will of course fail to provide an adequate defence, for the now familiar reasons. But suppose the passage is interpreted instead as suggesting that such restrictions constitute a rational response to the separateness of persons, even if they cannot be defended by appealing to the disvalue of violations. Is this suggestion more adequate? I think not. Though it avoids the fruitless appeal to the disvalue of violations, the proposal is defective for other reasons. The passage suggests that the rationality of agent-centred restrictions like R as a response to the separateness of persons derives from the fact that the violation of such a restriction harms some victim without compensating him for this harm. But the relevance of this fact is unclear. Why does this consideration make rational the view that it is wrong to violate such a restriction even in order to prevent a still greater number of equally weighty violations of the very same restriction? Whether A_1 harms P_1, in our schematic example, or A_2 . . . A_6 harm P_2 . . . P_6, *someone's* separate and distinct life will be violated without compensation. There is no question here of avoiding uncompensated violations altogether. The question instead is: why isn't it at least permissible to disrupt one distinct individual life, without compensation, in order to prevent the uncompensated disruption of five equally distinct lives? It is obviously no answer to this question to simply reiterate that

[10] *Anarchy, State, and Utopia*, pp. 32–3.

people are distinct, that each has only one life to lead, and that P_1 will not be compensated for the harm he suffers if A_1 violates R. This restatement provides no explanation whatsoever of the impermissibility of A_1's inflicting one uncompensated violation in order to prevent $A_2 \ldots A_6$ from inflicting five similarly uncompensated violations.

The problem with this particular attempt to motivate agent-centred restrictions like R is that it focuses on the possession of some allegedly significant property by the *victims* of violations. But agent-centred restrictions are restrictions which prohibit the victimizing of one person even to prevent the multiple victimization of other people, or comparably objectionable events. As noted in Chapter Two, the conceptual distinction to which such restrictions respond is the distinction between what would have the best overall outcome impersonally judged and what a person may permissibly do. And nothing one can say about the features of persons which make it undesirable for them to be victims will be capable of explaining a moral rule whose function is to deny that it is permissible to minimize equally undesirable victimizations. The question is not: what is it about people that makes it objectionable for them to be victimized? But rather: what is it about a person that makes it impermissible for him to victimize someone else even in order to minimize victimizations which are equally objectionable from an impersonal standpoint?

There is thus a general lesson to be learned from the failure of this particular attempt to motivate agent-centred restrictions like R. The lesson is that proposals to motivate agent-centred restrictions by construing them as a rational response to the possession of some allegedly significant property by the victims of violations, like proposals to motivate them by appealing to the *disvalue* of violations, are doomed to failure. Indeed, there is strong pressure for proposals of the first sort to collapse into proposals of the second sort. For if one tries to think of agent-centred restrictions as a rational response to the possession of some feature by the victims of violations, then it is natural to suppose, as I did in the last paragraph, that the feature in question must be one in virtue of which it is undesirable for persons to be victimized. And it is then only a short step to the

thought that the feature must be one in virtue of which violations are very bad things to have happen: one in virtue of which
they have very high disvalue. But whether or not proposals of
the first sort do in this way collapse into proposals of the second
sort, both types of proposals for motivating agent-centred
restrictions fail, and for just the same sorts of reasons. An appeal
to the disvalue of violations of such restrictions is powerless to
explain why one may not commit one violation in order to
prevent more numerous violations, of no less weight from an
impersonal standpoint, of the very same restriction, and hence
to avert an outcome with higher disvalue. An appeal to the
victims' possession of some property is powerless to explain why
one may not victimize one person with the feature in order to
prevent the victimization of still more people with the very same
feature. In each case, the appeal is to a consideration that
simply makes all violations of the restrictions seem equally
objectionable, and which thus appears to militate in favour of
permitting, rather than prohibiting, the minimization of total
overall violations. So, if there is to be an adequate rationale for
agent-centred restrictions, it cannot take the form of an appeal
to the victims' possession of some property, any more than it
can take the form of an appeal to the disvalue of violations.

It may be helpful at this point to review the direction in which
this search for a rationale for agent-centred restrictions has
been moving. I began by considering the idea that such restrictions can be motivated by appealing to the disvalue of their
violation. I concluded that they cannot be motivated through
an appeal to value any more than an agent-centred prerogative
can, and that any adequate rationale for the restrictions must
have a different form, just as the rationale for the prerogative
has a different form. I first considered, in this connection, the
possibility that the independence thesis is false, and that anyone who embraces the motivation for the agent-centred prerogative is thereby committed, on pain of inconsistency, to
accepting agent-centred restrictions as well. Having eventually
dismissed this possibility, I then considered the related but
distinct possibility that the restrictions, like the agent-centred
prerogative, represent all or part of *some* rational strategy for
responding to the independence of the personal point of view.

When that proposal also proved fruitless, it was suggested that the restrictions might instead be construed as a rational response to some *other* feature of persons. Consideration of the specific suggestion that restrictions against harming might be construed as a response to the *separateness* of persons led not only to the rejection of that particular suggestion, but also to the rejection of every other suggestion that tries to construe agent-centred restrictions as a rational response to the possession of some allegedly significant feature by the victims of violations. The possibility it seems natural to explore next is the possibility that such restrictions can be thought of as representing all or part of a rational response to the possession of some significant feature by agents who commit violations. We have already seen, of course, that they cannot be thought of as representing a rational response to the natural independence of the agent's point of view. But it may nevertheless be the case that they can be construed as a rational response to the possession by agents of some other feature. Indeed, since the restrictions, like the prerogative, introduce an agent-centred component into a moral theory—since the restrictions serve as a barrier between that which would have the best overall outcome impersonally judged and that which an agent may permissibly do—it is natural to suppose that the identification of a rationale for them must take the form of a demonstration that they represent a rational response to the agent's possession of *some* feature. If this suggestion should nevertheless prove as fruitless as the ones already considered, it may then be necessary to consider the possibility that there simply *is* no underlying principled rationale for the restrictions, and that the asymmetry thesis is thus true.

If agent-centred restrictions are to be thought of as embodying a rational response to the possession by agents of some significant property, what might the property in question be? A number of related suggestions come immediately to mind. It is often said, for instance, that an agent is specially responsible for what he does, and responsible only secondarily, if at all, for what he fails to prevent others from doing. The restrictions represent a rational response to this property of agents, it might be urged, for they hold that it is more important for an agent to avoid doing certain things than it is for him to prevent other people from doing equally objectionable things. Or, in a similar vein, it might be said that agents have a greater duty not to do certain things themselves than to prevent other people from doing the same things, and that agent-centred restrictions represent a rational response to *this* feature of persons.

Now the conceptions of individual responsibility and personal duty appealed to in these suggestions certainly constitute important components of those moral theories that include agent-centred restrictions. However, they cannot provide a rationale for the restrictions, for they stand as much in need of motivation as the restrictions themselves do. I made this point once before, in Chapter Two, when discussing the distinction between duties not to harm and duties to help, and it is worth making again. Trying to motivate agent-centred restrictions by construing them as a response to the 'fact' that people are more responsible for what they do than for what they fail to prevent is like trying to motivate an agent-centred prerogative by construing it as a response to the 'fact' that agents may devote energy and attention to their projects and plans out of proportion to the weight from the impersonal standpoint of their doing so. In each case, the proposal is to motivate a moral rule by appealing to a moral doctrine which the rule enforces. Agent-centred restrictions serve to enforce the moral view that individuals are more responsible for what they do than for what they fail to prevent; relative to a moral conception that includes such restrictions, in other words, individuals *are* (morally) more responsible for what they do than for what they fail to prevent. Similarly, an agent-centred prerogative serves to enforce the moral view that individuals may devote energy and attention to their projects and commitments out of proportion to the weight from the impersonal standpoint of their doing so; relative to a moral conception that includes an agent-centred prerogative, agents *may*, morally, devote energy and attention to their projects and commitments out of proportion to the weight from the impersonal standpoint of their doing so.

But, quite obviously, we are striving to understand the motivation for the moral doctrines in question as much as for the rules which enforce them. In each case, doctrine and rule constitute two sides of the same coin, and it is the choice of coin we wish to understand. In the search for a motivation for an agent-centred prerogative, the aim was to understand *why* it should be thought that agents may devote energy and attention to their projects and plans out of proportion to the weight from the impersonal standpoint of their doing so. It proved possible to answer this question by showing that this moral doctrine, and the rules which enforce it, constitute a rational response to the independence of the personal point of view. In searching now for a motivation for agent-centred restrictions, similarly, the aim is to understand *why* an individual's responsibility to avoid doing certain things should be thought so great as to outweigh the good that would be achieved by preventing still more people from doing the very same objectionable things. It may or may not be possible to find a satisfactory answer to this question. But it is clear in any case that appeals to personal duty and personal responsibility cannot provide a rationale of the desired sort for the restrictions, for they are part and parcel of the moral view whose motivation is in question.

A revised proposal might be to think of agent-centred restrictions like R, together with accompanying conceptions of personal responsibility and personal duty, as constituting one rational response to the fact that human beings have the capacity to directly cause harm to other human beings. This proposal would appeal in the appropriate way to the possession of some allegedly significant property by human agents. And unlike the previous suggestion, it would not appeal to a property whose ascription to individuals is part of the very moral doctrine whose motivation is in question. Instead, this suggestion would seek to construe that doctrine itself as part of a rational response to a property that agents uncontroversially possess. The proposal might be elaborated as follows. Just as there may be more than one rational strategy for responding to the natural independence of the personal point of view, so too there may be several rational responses to the fact that human beings have the capacity to perform actions which directly cause harm to other human beings. One strategy is to prohibit all actions of this sort absolutely, and this is the strategy embodied by fully agent-centred conceptions.[11] Other strategies may also be rational. But, assuming that such actions are indeed thought of as objectionable, surely it is evident that a strategy that prohibits them all is at least *one* rational strategy.

The strategy of prohibiting all actions which directly harm others may *sound* rational, but it is not clear that it is in fact rational. Notice that a strategy which required the *minimization* of such actions would agree with the strategy of complete prohibition to the extent of forbidding all such actions *other than* those which would minimize the total number of actions of the same kind. Thus complete prohibition is a 'first-order' component of both of these strategies, in the following sense: if everyone were to obey the rules embodying either strategy, then *no* actions that directly harm others would be performed. Both strategies agree that their *first* choice is for nobody to perform such actions. They disagree only on *second-order* strategy: on what to instruct agents to do in case *some* people have violated the rules embodying the first-order prohibition, or seem likely to do so. A strategy that requires minimization has as its second choice that people act so as to ensure that as few of the actions that directly harm others be performed as possible. Thus this strategy prefers that no such actions be performed, and failing that, it prefers that people act in such a way as to ensure that as few such actions as possible are performed. On its face, *this* strategy seems to be a rational one. The strategy of complete prohibition, by contrast, incorporates a second-order strategy which prohibits the performance of actions that directly harm others even when these actions would minimize the total number of actions of the very same kind. As a result, this strategy in effect has as its first choice that nobody should commit such actions, and as its second choice that people should *not* act in such a way as to ensure that as few such actions as possible are performed. The rationality of *this* strategy is not evident. For it is not evident why, if such actions are so

[11] Clearly this is an overstatement. Properly speaking, only those fully agent-centred conceptions which are 'absolutist' could really be said to embody a *complete* prohibition strategy. Thus if such a strategy were indeed rational, non-absolutists would need to explain their departures from complete prohibition.

objectionable as to be completely prohibited by first-order strategy, their minimization should be positively forbidden by second-order strategy. Pending a satisfactory answer to that question, agent-centred restrictions like R cannot be said to represent a demonstrably rational response to the fact that people have the capacity to directly inflict harm on each other.

One way of trying to improve on the last proposal, so as to avoid the difficulty it encountered, is by attempting to construe agent-centred restrictions like R as a rational response to the fact that people have the capacity to *intentionally* cause harm to others. The intentionality of intentional harms may be thought to be important because it seems to bespeak a fundamental lack of respect for the person who is victimized. And it may be felt that, given this construal of the significance of intentional harms, a strategy of completely prohibiting such harms may indeed be rational. In other words, the added element of intentionality may be thought to make a complete prohibition strategy seem rational in a way that the previous proposal was unable to. In this vein, Charles Fried writes:

The two elements, intention and doing harm, may be seen as picturing a relation between a moral agent and the object of his agency, a relation which is inconsistent with the basic notion of respect for persons. And that inconsistency explains why the prohibition is categorical. The absolute norm is grounded in the importance to us of our physical integrity and in the special evil of a relation established between people in which one person exercises his peculiarly human efficacy to attack another's physical integrity. It is just because the person of the victim is threatened by the person of the actor that the relation has a special moral significance. From the victim's perspective, to be hurt by a natural force or by accident is different from being the object of an intentional attack, even though the actual injury may be identical. The intention makes for the offense.[12]

The heart of this proposal is the claim that the inconsistency of an intentional harm with the notion of respect for persons explains the rationality of the kind of complete prohibition strategy which fully agent-centred conceptions embody. The persuasiveness of this claim depends on the persuasiveness of the alleged explanation it refers to. How exactly does the inconsistency between intentional harm and respect for persons

[12] *Right and Wrong* (Harvard University Press, 1978), pp. 31–2.

explain the rationality of a complete prohibition strategy? Such a strategy, remember, prohibits a person from performing an action of the objectionable kind even when doing so would minimize the total number of actions of the very same kind. And the rationality of this strategy, it seems to me, is still not evident. For it remains obscure why, if intentional harms are so objectionable as to be completely prohibited by first-order strategy, their minimization should be positively forbidden by second-order strategy. It is obviously no answer to this question to simply claim that any minimizing harm must itself be a violation of respect for persons. For even if that is so (and it is far from obvious that it is), it is also the case that any such action must serve to minimize the total number of instances of comparable disrespect for persons. And the idea that an intentional harm manifests objectionable disrespect for persons hardly explains why one must not act in such a way as to ensure that there are as few such manifestations as possible.

So far, then, no underlying principled rationale for agent-centred restrictions has been indentified. I myself do not see what an adequate rationale for such restrictions might be. Of course, there may nevertheless be such a rationale. But as matters now stand, there is every reason to take the asymmetry thesis seriously.

The defender of agent-centred restrictions may remind us that hybrid conceptions, like fully agent-centred conceptions, do not systematically require the production of the best overall states of affairs. Thus both types of conception are willing to tolerate avoidable instances of objectionable happenings in the world. So why, he may ask, is this willingness deemed rational for hybrid conceptions but not for fully agent-centred conceptions? The answer, it is important to remember, is this. Hybrid conceptions do not systematically *require* the production of the best overall states of affairs, because by not doing so they are able to reflect the natural independence of the personal point of view. But it is not clear what, analogously, is accomplished by not *permitting* the production of the best states of affairs. And as long as that remains unclear, the rationality of agent-centred restrictions remains in question.

The defender of agent-centred restrictions may say, at this

point, that whatever the difficulties involved in identifying a rationale for the restrictions, it is nevertheless the case that any moral conception that fails to include them will have absolutely unacceptable features. Admittedly, he may say, it has proved difficult to identify an underlying rationale for the restrictions, and these difficulties may lead some people to suspect that the restrictions are rationally indefensible despite their intuitive appeal. But the discussion so far has failed to show just how strong the intuitive appeal of such restrictions can be. For the discussion has focused on cases of a sort exemplified by the schematic example in which, if A_1 fails to violate R by harming P_1, five other agents will identically harm $P_2 \ldots P_6$. And there are other sorts of cases in which the intuitive appeal of the restrictions is even greater. In reflecting on cases of this other kind, it becomes clear that rejecting the restrictions is simply unacceptable.

This argument might be developed more fully as follows. Consider a case in which killing one innocent person is the only way to prevent, not five identical killings, but the *deaths* of five other people by accident or disease. Most people would say, without hesitation, that it would be impermissible in such a case to kill the innocent person. Clearly, a fully agent-centred conception can accommodate this view; a rule against killing the innocent, except perhaps in the most extreme circumstances, would presumably yield the desired prohibition. But it is not at all clear that a conception that rejects agent-centred restrictions has any plausible way to forbid killing in a case such as this. It appears that defenders of consequentialist and hybrid conceptions have only two approaches they can take with regard to examples of this kind. First, they can simply insist that, if other consequential considerations are equal, then it *is* permissible to kill the one person in order to save the five (or even, the consequentialist may say, required). Second, they can suggest that one killing is a worse thing to happen than five deaths caused by accident or disease, and hence that killing the innocent person is prohibited because it actually produces the worse overall outcome.

Both of these responses, it may be said, are unacceptable. The first does violence to one of our firmest moral convictions.

The second requires a highly implausible account of the good. For a killing is not a worse thing to happen than *one* otherwise equally undesirable death, let alone a worse thing than five such deaths. It is not very plausible to maintain that, if the amount of suffering is held constant, a person who is killed suddenly and unexpectedly has had something worse happen to him than what would have happened to him had he died by sudden accident or disease at the same point in his life. This suggests, as T. M. Scanlon has put it, 'that the distinctive moral badness of killings compared with other deaths exists, if at all, only in an agent-centred morality focusing on what you *do*. Once we move to the moral appraisal of what *happens*, the differential treatment of killings and otherwise equally undesirable deaths becomes much less plausible'.[13] The force of this point may be brought home through an example. Consider two twins, equally innocent. While we are strongly inclined to say that it would be impermissible to kill the first twin in order to prevent the accidental death of the second twin, even if that were the only way to prevent the second twin's death, we have no comparably strong inclination to say that it would be impermissible to prevent the accidental death of the second twin instead of preventing the murder of the first twin by some other person, if one could only prevent the death or the killing but not both. This asymmetry in our reactions lends support to the claim that the differential treatment of killings and other equally undesirable deaths is not especially plausible in the context of a moral appraisal of what happens.

Thus, the defender of agent-centred restrictions may argue, in a case of the kind we have been considering, opponents of the restrictions can only say one of two things. Either they can take the unacceptable position that it is permissible to kill the one person in order to save the five from accidental death, or they can take the highly implausible position that, killings being at least five times worse than accidental deaths, killing the one person is impermissible because it leads to the worse overall outcome. In contrast, someone who accepts agent-centred restrictions can agree, plausibly, that the overall outcome of not

[13] Personal communication: October 1976.

killing the person would be at least as bad as the overall outcome of killing, while at the same time insisting, sensibly, that it is impermissible to kill. And, the argument may conclude, the intuitions to which agent-centred restrictions thus respond, in examples of this kind, are so secure, that they provide ample reason to accept the restrictions despite the difficulties encountered in attempting to identify a principled rationale for them.

Obviously, the foregoing argument relies heavily on the intuition that it is impermissible to kill one person in order to prevent more numerous deaths due to accident or disease. And the first point to be made, in response to the argument, is that this intuition itself appears to be informed to a considerable extent by consequential considerations. The world has known all too many people whose zeal for killing has not been matched by any great talent for accurately predicting the consequences of their actions, and all too many killers whose judgements about what ends are valuable have been deranged, biased, self-serving, or otherwise misguided.[14] These considerations based on experience, which Scanlon calls considerations of 'mistrust',[15] contribute substantially to the intuitions that the argument in behalf of agent-centred restrictions appeals to. But these considerations are consequential in character. We fear for the consequences if everyone were to view himself as having the moral authority to kill any time killing would, in his considered judgement, produce the best available state of affairs overall. We fear that the world would become an awful place. And our fear for the consequences is naturally greater when we contemplate what the world would be like if people were to view themselves as having the moral authority to kill for the purpose of minimizing deaths of any kind than it is when we

[14] Compare M. Walzer:

Unfortunately, there are always going to be soldiers on the battlefields of Blenheim who think they are standing at Armageddon and who are prepared to risk some awful crime for the sake of victory. That is why moral rules are so important and why they are usually stated and probably should be stated (in international law, for example) in absolute terms.

('World War II: Why Was This War Different?' in *War and Moral Responsibility*, M. Cohen, T. Nagel, and T. Scanlon, eds. (Princeton University Press, 1974), at p. 103.)

[15] 'Rights, Goals, and Fairness', in *Public and Private Morality*, S. Hampshire, ed. (Cambridge University Press, 1978), at p. 109.

contemplate people viewing themselves as having the moral authority to kill only to minimize killings. For the first kind of authority is much broader than the second, and since we rightly fear the way in which the presumed moral authority to kill may be wielded under any circumstances, our fear for the consequences is naturally stronger when we contemplate such authority being wielded more broadly.

Just because these considerations are consequential in character, however, defenders of consequentialist and hybrid conceptions can and must take them into account. If a killing that will minimize deaths in the short run will also significantly increase the likelihood of unjustified killings in the long run, then that is something that may well count decisively against the original killing, from the point of view of these conceptions. So to the extent that our intuitions about the impermissibility of such killings are intuitions about consequences, those who accept consequentialist and hybrid conceptions can accommodate them without claiming that a killing is in itself a worse thing to happen than an otherwise equally undesirable death.

Suppose, however, that these consequential considerations were drained from the picture. Suppose that there was a machine, the Infallible Optimizer, which never made mistakes in its judgements about which of the actions available to an agent at a time would actually minimize total deaths overall. Suppose further that people were causally incapable of killing unless the Infallible Optimizer certified that a killing was necessary in order to minimize total deaths. Defenders of agent-centred restrictions will presumably feel a residual intuition that, even under circumstances such as these, it would be wrong to kill a person in order to minimize deaths. To this intuition, it seems to me, those who reject the restrictions can respond as follows. Either the intuition *is*, arguments to the contrary notwithstanding, an intuition that such killings are worse things to happen than deaths, in which case it can be accommodated in the evaluation of outcomes, or it is an intuition that such killings are impermissible even though the more numerous deaths that will result from failing to kill constitute at least as bad an outcome as one killing, in which case it need not be accommodated, pending some account of the underlying principled motivation from which it springs. Drained of its consequential component, the intuition that one must not commit one killing in order to prevent five equally bad things from happening remains an intuition in search of a foundation.[16]

But, it may be said, don't all ethical convictions rest ultimately on intuitions which themselves have no further foundation? In some sense, perhaps; but even if so, it is still possible to inquire into the *level* at which a moral conception's foundational intuitions arise, and into the compatibility of those intuitions with canons of rationality. The agent-centred prerogative, as we have seen, is responsive to some strong and widely shared intuitions. But in addition, it has proved possible to identify underlying general convictions from which those surface intuitions emerge. In the case of agent-centred restrictions, by contrast, we have only the surface intuitions; no underlying general rationale has yet been identified. Of course, as I have emphasized, it has not been conclusively shown that there exists no underlying rationale for agent-centred restrictions. And even if there were no such rationale, many people would doubtless feel that the intuitions to which the restrictions respond are nevertheless so central that they cannot in the end be rejected, problematic though they may be. Nothing I have said has established conclusively that such a view would be irrational, or absolutely unacceptable for other reasons. But unless it is possible to identify an underlying rationale for the restrictions, I do think that those who accept them have serious cause for concern.

For, first, the persistent air of paradox surrounding the restrictions creates the impression that they may be intrinsically flawed from a rational point of view. Second, the fact that it is possible to identify an underlying general source for the concerns to which the agent-centred prerogative responds tends to make the restrictions look poorly motivated *relatively* speaking, thus reinforcing the suspicion that they may be rationally indefensible. And third, it is only too easy to think of a psychological explanation for the commitment to agent-centred restrictions, an explanation that would provide a motivation of

[16] For a related discussion, see John Harris, 'The Survival Lottery', *Philosophy* 50 (1975): 81–7.

a kind for the restrictions, but not a motivation that would make them seem especially well-founded morally. More specifically, the commitment to agent-centred restrictions may represent what Scanlon calls the 'bias of the lucky against the unlucky'.[17] Even if an Infallible Optimizer could guarantee that the rejection of agent-centred restrictions would result in the minimization of the total *overall* number of injuries and untimely deaths, some people might feel that *their own* chances of avoiding such misfortunes are actually better with the restrictions than they would be without them. For due to their own favourable circumstances and private resources, which the restrictions serve to protect, they have a much higher than average chance of warding off misfortunes in a society where the operative moral conception includes such restrictions. Under a scheme that rejected the restrictions, however, they would, without compensating advantages, be exposed to an additional form of risk: the risk that harming them or undermining their favourable circumstances might be a morally acceptable way for someone to promote the overall good. Thus although the total number of overall misfortunes might be minimized, *their* chances of experiencing such a misfortune might increase, just as a radical redistribution of wealth, which minimized the total number of poor people in a society, might also increase the chances of poverty for some who were extremely well-off before the re-distribution. The rejection of agent-centred restrictions accomplishes a redistribution of moral protection, and one source of our reluctance to reject the restrictions may be a sense that we are among those with the most to lose in such a redistribution.[18] Of course, the rejection of an agent-centred prerogative also accomplishes a redistribution of moral protection. I have tried to suggest, however, that the reluctance to reject such a prerogative may not be rooted simply in self-interest. For the prerogative, unlike the restrictions, appears to have an independent principled rationale; it represents one rational response to the natural independence of the personal point of view.

[17] 'Rights, Goals, and Fairness', at p. 109.
[18] For a related discussion, see Gilbert Harman, *The Nature of Morality* (New York: Oxford University Press, 1977), pp. 110–11.

Thus although an ultimate failure to identify an underlying principled rationale for agent-centred restrictions might not in itself constitute a decisive argument against the restrictions, it would indeed provide cause for serious concern. I have no doubt that many readers of these pages will find themselves, as I find myself in certain moods, more impressed by the particular intuitions to which the restrictions respond than by the general difficulties encountered in attempting to motivate them, and that these people will continue to accept the restrictions despite those difficulties. But, at the same time, I hope these readers will also agree that there are reasons to be worried about agent-centred restrictions, and feel challenged to identify that rationale for the restrictions which has so far eluded our grasp.

5

THE PROJECT RECONSIDERED

LET me review the course of the investigation to this point. I began by taking note of utilitarianism's surprising persistence in the face of widespread criticism, and by suggesting, in a preliminary way, that the persistence of utilitarianism may stem from the fact that, as the most familiar consequentialist moral theory, it is the major recognized normative theory incorporating the plausible-sounding idea that one may always do what would lead to the best outcome overall. Standard deontological conceptions, I noted, reject that idea. They hold not only that one is not always required to produce the best available states of affairs overall, but also that it is sometimes positively impermissible to do so. Given the intuitive plausibility of the idea that one may always do what would have the best outcome, and given the prima-facie difficulties associated with those moral conceptions that do not accept that idea, I was led to reconsider the rejection of consequentialism.

More specifically, I was led to undertake a comparative examination of two different kinds of non-consequentialist moral conceptions: hybrid conceptions, which depart from consequentialism to the extent of incorporating an agent-centred prerogative, and which thus hold that one is always permitted but not always required to do what would have the best available outcome overall, and fully agent-centred conceptions, which incorporate both an agent-centred prerogative and agent-centred restrictions, and which thus hold that one is neither required nor permitted always to do what would have the best outcome. The examination revealed that although both the agent-centred prerogative and agent-centred restrictions are responsive to anti-consequentialist intuitions of one sort or another, it is much easier to identify an underlying principled rationale for the former than for the latter. Thus as between the two sorts of non-consequentialist moral conceptions, hybrid conceptions seemed to emerge from the examination with a kind of relative advantage. For, unlike fully agent-centred conceptions, they retain the initially plausible consequentialist idea that it is always permissible to do what would lead to the best overall outcome, while at the same time accommodating those anti-consequentialist intuitions that do seem theoretically well-founded. I concluded that although many people will continue to feel that agent-centred restrictions are indispensable, there are good reasons, in the absence of a plausible principled rationale for such restrictions, to worry about the adequacy of moral conceptions that include them.

Before resting content with this conclusion, however, it is important to reconsider the structure of the overall investigation, as just described, in order to make sure that that investigation itself has not been poorly conceived. Defenders of agent-centred restrictions might try to show that it has. They might try to show that, for one reason or another, our search for a rationale for the restrictions has been inappropriate, and in this way to discredit the results of that search. For example, it might be argued that the very idea of ranking overall states of affairs is misguided, and that therefore no special rationale is required for the restrictions which prohibit doing what would produce 'the best state of affairs overall'. If this argument could be made persuasively, it would presumably show that our search for a rationale for agent-centred restrictions has been inappropriate, and that there is therefore nothing troublesome about the lack of success met with on that search. But, in my view, the argument cannot be made persuasively. I believe, more specifically, that the idea of ranking overall states of affairs is not misguided, and that even if it were, it would still be appropriate to seek an underlying principled rationale for agent-centred restrictions. These claims need to be defended carefully.

Someone who believed that the idea of ranking overall states of affairs was misguided might argue in the following way.

Human interests by their nature are not the sorts of things that can be balanced interpersonally to yield a unified evaluation. There are only individual lives and there are, ultimately, only individual harms and benefits. An individual's suffering is finally and irredeemably his suffering, and it cannot change character by virtue of coexisting with benefits to other people. To weigh, balance, or blend the suffering of one person against or with the experiences of other people, is to presuppose what is not true: that human pains are individually measurable, interpersonally comparable, and ultimately compensable from the standpoint of eternity.

This argument, that the willingness to rank overall states of affairs presupposes a false view about the possibility of interpersonal compensation,[1] seems to me unpersuasive. The judgement that one state of affairs is better than another is consistent with the recognition that some people may suffer terribly even in the better state of affairs. Such a judgement in no way presupposes that those sufferings are neutralized, erased, or compensated for by virtue of the fact that they form part of one overall state of affairs that is deemed better than some other overall state of affairs. What such a judgement does involve is simply the belief that one overall pattern of benefits and harms is better than another, taking full account of the fact that in each case some of the harms may not admit of compensation. Individual harms are set in their larger context for the purpose of rendering judgements about the relative merits of overall states of affairs, and since from the standpoint of those judgements the larger pattern of harms and benefits is decisive, a harm that is awful to suffer and is in no way compensated for may nevertheless be said to fall within the best available state of affairs. Clearly, the plausibility of particular judgements about the relative merits of overall states of affairs will depend on the plausibility of the principle used to compare overall patterns of benefits and burdens. In the last chapter, I presented a

---

[1] Recall that in Chapter Four (at pp. 98–100) I considered and rejected the suggestion that the impossibility of interpersonal compensation for harm might provide a rationale in certain circumstances for prohibiting the production of the best states of affairs. The alternative suggestion here is that the very idea of ranking overall states of affairs may rest on a confusion about the possibility of interpersonal compensation for harm.

rationale for preferring a distribution-sensitive ranking principle to the principle of comparison employed by classical utilitarianism. But while there may be disagreements about the appropriate principle to rely on, it is clear enough that we are familiar with assessments of the relative merits of overall states of affairs. Indeed, we are required to make them in all kinds of circumstances. Some of the most important problems of social choice and social decision revolve around competing judgements of this form, and to refrain from making such judgements is to pretend that there is no ground for preferring any one outcome to any other, from a moral point of view.

Someone who believed that the idea of ranking overall states of affairs was misguided might try to argue for that belief in another way. Consider two states of affairs, A and B. In A, one person dies an undesirable death. In B, five other people die equally undesirable deaths. There are no other relevant differences between A and B. Now, it might be said, it only makes sense to call A a better state of affairs than B if one holds the mistaken belief that the deaths of five individual people can be summed into one mass death which is five times worse than ordinary death: that the deaths of five individuals are somehow equivalent to one person dying five times, or five times as intensely. This view about the additive nature of harms is clearly confused. For obviously, '[f]ive individuals each losing his life does not add up to anyone's experiencing a loss five times greater than the loss suffered by any one of the five'.[2] But only if someone *were* experiencing a loss five times greater than the loss suffered by any one of the five would it make sense to say that A was a better state of affairs than B. For judgements of value only make sense relative to the experience of some being. Since nobody is experiencing a fivefold loss, it makes no sense to say that A is better than B.

---

[2] John Taurek, 'Should the Numbers Count?', *Philosophy and Public Affairs* 6 (1977): 293–316, at p. 307. The argument under consideration, that the commitment to ranking overall states of affairs rests on a confusion about the experiential additivity of harms, was suggested to me by Taurek's paper. However, I have formulated the argument somewhat differently than he does, and I do not discuss his paper directly. Such discussion can be found in Derek Parfit, 'Innumerate Ethics', *Philosophy and Public Affairs* 7 (1978): 285–301, and in the exchange of correspondence between Parfit and Charles Fried, *Philosophy and Public Affairs* 8 (1979): 393–7. I have greatly profited from discussions of Taurek's paper with T. M. Scanlon.

This argument, as it stands, appears to be compatible with a limited principle for ranking overall outcomes, to the effect that an outcome X is better than an outcome Y if and only if the worst-harmed individual in X is less severely harmed than the worst-harmed individual in Y.[3] And to the extent that the argument is incompatible with rankings that are sensitive to differences in the mere *numbers* of people who experience harms of given magnitudes, the argument seems to me mistaken. In order to hold that, other things equal, it is a better thing if ten children are saved from imminent starvation than if one is, it is not necessary to illicitly suppose that some multiply emaciated being will starve ten times over if the one child is favoured. Nor does the judgement cease to make sense if it does *not* rest on an illicit supposition of this kind. It seems not at all senseless to assert that, other things equal, it is better that fewer people should suffer rather than more, better that more should prosper rather than fewer. Better that five people should die of smallpox than that a million should, better that a million children should receive the benefits of an adequate diet or a decent education or protection against polio than that five should. This seems to me the common sense, and I see no reason to reject it. I see no reason to think either that judgements of this form tacitly and illicitly appeal to the idea of a unique subject who suffers harms aggregatively, or that we should abstain from making such judgements once we recognize that they do not so appeal. Where the relative merits of two overall states of affairs are concerned, a larger number of discrete harms of magnitude M can 'dominate' a smaller number of such harms, even though nobody suffers the larger number of harms aggregatively.

Thus the idea of ranking overall states of affairs does not rest on a mistaken belief about the possibility of interpersonal compensation for harm or about the experiental additivity of harms. Moreover, even if one did reject the idea of ranking overall

[3] John Campbell has suggested to me that the argument may be compatible only with a more limited ranking principle, according to which an outcome X is better than an outcome Y if and only if the worst-harmed person in X is less severely harmed than the *least*-harmed person in Y. To put it another way, an outcome X is better than an outcome Y, on this view, if and only if it is the case that *whichever* person in X one chooses and *whichever* person in Y one chooses, the person in X is less severely harmed than the person in Y.

states of affairs, the search for a rationale for agent-centred restrictions would still be just as well-motivated as it is otherwise. For the apparently problematic features of such restrictions—the features that lend a sense of urgency to the search for a rationale—are independent of the idea of ranking overall states of affairs, and persist even if that idea is rejected. An agent-centred restriction, as we have seen, is a restriction that it is at least sometimes impermissible to violate in circumstances where doing so would prevent either more numerous violations, of no less weight from an impersonal standpoint, of the very same restriction, or other equally objectionable events, and where there are no other morally relevant consequences to be considered. And even if the idea of ranking overall states of affairs is rejected, Nozick's question still arises: why aren't agent-centred restrictions irrational? How can it be rational to maintain that the minimization of objectionable occurrences is wrong? So long as the rationality of such restrictions remains in question, the request for a rationale remains in order.

To summarize, I have argued that the idea of ranking overall states of affairs is not misguided, and that even if it were, that would not count against the appropriateness of seeking an underlying principled rationale for agent-centred restrictions. Anyone who hopes to demonstrate that the demand for a rationale for the constraints is inappropriate will have to produce some different and better argument.

One attempt to provide such an argument might be developed along the following lines. The demand for a rationale for agent-centred restrictions, it might be said, contains a concealed bias against such restrictions. For, the argument might continue, the presumption has been that there is a prima-facie plausibility about the consequentialist conception of the right, and that departures from consequentialism thus need special justification. But this presumption is question-begging. Those who accept fully agent-centred moral conceptions might just as well assert that there is a prima-facie plausibility about the view of right action embodied by *those* conceptions, and that it is departures from them that therefore require special justification. The two claims are exactly parallel; they beg the same question in opposite directions. And it is no help to say that departures from consequentialism require special justification because consequentialism incorporates the plausible-sounding idea that one may always do what would lead to the best overall outcome. For one might just as easily say that departures from fully agent-centred conceptions require special justification because such conceptions incorporate the plausible-sounding idea that one must not do what would be wrong. Thus, the argument might conclude, the demand for a rationale for agent-centred restrictions is not one that those who accept the restrictions need take seriously, for it arises out of a prejudicial antecedent belief in the presumptive plausibility of consequentialism.

This line of thought seems to me mistaken, but it is important to see exactly where and how it goes wrong. A first response to the argument might be to criticize its suggestion that a rationale for agent-centred restrictions has been thought necessary only because such restrictions represent a departure from consequentialism. In the first place, the salient features of *all* moral conceptions stand in need of principled motivation. Although I have been devoting most of my attention to possible considerations underlying an agent-centred prerogative and agent-centred restrictions, it is certainly legitimate to ask for a rationale for the consequentialist conception of the right. In the second place, agent-centred restrictions, as we have seen, have certain apparently paradoxical features. And, as I have emphasized, the apparent irrationality of the restrictions does not consist simply in the fact that they represent a departure from consequentialism. Indeed, as I have already indicated, the apparently problematic features of agent-centred restrictions can be described without even mentioning consequentialism or the idea of doing what would lead to the best overall outcome. And without any antecedent bias in favour of consequentialism, it is natural to wonder whether there is some underlying principled motivation for the restrictions which is capable of dispelling the air of irrationality that surrounds them. The idea that it is objectionable to act in such a way as to minimize objectionable acts is problematic in its own right, and this fact provides reason enough to ask what the motivation for agent-centred restrictions might be.

Moreover, although it is legitimate in any case to ask for a rationale for the consequentialist conception of the right, it is noteworthy that this conception has no comparable paradoxical feature, so it is simply not true that all the reasons for seeking a rationale for agent-centred restrictions are paralleled by equally weighty reasons for seeking a rationale for the consequentialist view of right action. Similarly, there is an important difference between the plausible-sounding idea that the argument under consideration attributes to fully agent-centred conceptions, and the plausible-sounding idea that I have attributed to consequentialism. It is completely trivial to say that fully agent-centred conceptions incorporate the idea that one must not do what is wrong. *All* moral conceptions, consequentialist and non-consequentialist alike, incorporate that idea; what they disagree about is the nature and content of the wrong. An idea that captures what all moral conceptions agree on and remains silent on the issues that divide them cannot properly be associated with any one conception rather than any other. It is not similarly trivial to say that consequentialism incorporates the idea that one may always do what would lead to the best overall outcome. For it is not true that all moral conceptions incorporate *this* idea; as we have seen, fully agent-centred conceptions reject it. Thus the supposed parallel drawn here is as spurious as the supposed parallel between the reasons for seeking a rationale for agent-centred restrictions and the reasons for seeking a rationale for the consequentialist conception of the right. There is, I conclude, no reason to accept the claim that the search for a rationale for the restrictions arises out of a prejudicial antecedent belief in the presumptive plausibility of consequentialism.

Although this response suffices to rebut the claim that the demand for a rationale for agent-centred restrictions is prejudicial and hence inappropriate, it also acknowledges that the underlying rationale for the consequentialist conception of the right has not yet been explicitly examined. And despite the fact that consequentialist moral conceptions do incorporate the plausible idea that one may always do what would lead to the best overall outcome and do not have the paradoxical quality of fully agent-centred conceptions, it may be thought that it is premature to draw any negative conclusions about the rationale for agent-centred restrictions until the rationale for the consequentialist conception of the right is explained. For, it may be thought, once the rationale for that conception is at hand, it may be evident that an equally satisfactory rationale is available for the restrictions after all.

In order to forestall this sort of criticism, it is important to say something explicit about the rationale for the consequentialist conception of the right. The consequentialist, it seems to me, reasons as follows. The theory of the right takes as its starting point the fact that people are not indifferent about what happens in the world; on the contrary, there are happenings that people regard as good and happenings they regard as bad. If people were not sensitive in this way to differences in what happens, there would be no need for a conception of the right as ordinarily thought of. For if people did not make these discriminations, and there was thus no way that human actions could cause or constitute occurrences that people regarded as good or bad, then there would be no need to regulate human action in the way that a conception of the right does. Since the need for a conception of the right to regulate human conduct arises in this way from the fact that people are not indifferent about what happens, the principles of right action should embody a rational way of regulating what happens, in so far as that is subject to human control. And it is hard to see how any conception of the right could embody a more rational way of doing this than the consequentialist conception, which requires agents to promote the best overall states of affairs, and hence, in effect, to promote the best overall sets of happenings in the world.

Different consequentialist theories, of course, incorporate different principles for ranking overall states of affairs, and hence embody different conceptions of what it is best to have happen in the world. But all consequentialist theories incorporate the same conception of the right, which requires the production of the best overall states of affairs. And the motivation for that conception of the right is that it represents a rational way of regulating what happens in the world, in so far as what happens is subject to human control. Bearing these points in mind, the 'sophisticated' consequentialist's response to the natural independence of the personal point of view, discussed in Chapter Three, can now be put in broader perspective. Recall that the sophisticated consequentialist regards the independence of the personal point of view as important primarily for the influence it exerts on the constitution of the individual good, and responds by insisting, roughly, that each agent should act in such a way as to maximize the number of individuals who are actually achieving their good so conceived, and the degree to which each is achieving it. And recall that in view of the apparent rationality of this response to personal independence, it was suggested in Chapter Three that the sophisticated consequentialist might propose as a motivation for sophisticated consequentialism as a whole that it embodies a rational strategy for taking account of the nature of a person as a being with an independent point of view. Now, however, we can see that it would be misleading to present this as an account of the ultimate motivation for sophisticated consequentialism. For the sophisticated consequentialist's response to personal independence is itself the outgrowth of a conviction that the best thing to have happen in the world is for the good of human individuals, properly understood and rationally aggregated, to be advanced to the greatest extent possible, together with a conviction that a conception of the right should represent a rational way of regulating what happens in the world. Thus the ultimate motivation for sophisticated consequentialism as a whole is not that it embodies a rational strategy for responding to the natural independence of the personal point of view, but instead is simply the conjunction of the motivations for its several elements: its account of the individual good, its account of the overall good, and the account of the right which it shares with other consequentialist theories. And the motivation for that conception of the right, as we have now seen, is not that *it* embodies a rational response to any one particular natural fact, but rather that it represents a rational way of regulating what happens in the world, in so far as what happens is within human control.

We can now appreciate a fundamental difference between

the consequentialist conception of the right and the one embodied by hybrid conceptions. Any conception of the right attempts to regulate the conduct of agents, and also to thereby regulate what happens in the world, in so far as what happens is subject to human control. But the consequentialist conception of the right embodies a conviction that the second of these functions should take priority over the first. That is, the best principles for regulating the conduct of agents will be those principles, whatever they are, which represent the most rational way of regulating what happens. After all, the consequentialist reasons, it is only because people care about what happens that a conception of the right is needed in the first place. So the consequentialist first fixes on a principle for identifying the best available states of affairs, or the best available sets of happenings, and then simply directs agents to do what is in their power to produce those states of affairs or sets of happenings.

Hybrid conceptions, by contrast, embody a conviction that it is wrong-headed to allow the principles of human conduct to be completely determined by an antecedently fixed conception of what the best overall sets of happenings would be. Although there might be no need for a conception of the right if people did not care about what happened, it is nevertheless the case that a conception of the right can attempt to regulate what happens *only* in so far as what happens is subject to human control. The happenings that a conception of the right attempts to regulate are those that depend on the actions of human agents. And to someone who accepts a hybrid view, this suggests a constraint on the way in which an adequate conception of the right can seek to regulate what happens. That is, such a conception must first of all embody a set of demands that it is reasonable to make of human agents. And there may be features of human agents in virtue of which it is rational to require of them something other than the constant production of the best states of affairs or the best overall sets of happenings. In particular, of course, those who accept hybrid conceptions believe that, given one construal of the importance of the natural independence of the personal point of view, it is rational to allow people to devote energy and attention to their projects and plans out of proportion to the weight in the impersonal calculus of their doing so.

Although the position articulated on behalf of hybrid conceptions seems to me the more appealing of the two, I will not try to resolve this dispute between hybrid and consequentialist views. Enough has been said by now, I hope, to show that hybrid conceptions are worthy of serious attention, and that is what I set out to establish. As I have indicated before, it has not been my intention to argue that hybrid conceptions are categorically superior to consequentialist theories. I prefer to leave open the question whether this is so, and with it the question whether it is even appropriate to suppose that there is a single, objectively superior moral conception. My inquiry has been confined to an attempt to identify comprehensible motivations for the salient features of different types of moral conceptions, and my central argument has been that it is much easier to identify a rationale for one kind of non-consequentialist moral feature than for another: much easier to identify a rationale for an agent-centred prerogative than for agent-centred restrictions. If I am right about this, then not only do the relatively unfamiliar conceptions I have been calling 'hybrid conceptions' need to be taken very seriously, but the more familiar deontological views I have been calling 'fully agent-centred conceptions' may seem especially problematic. The primary reason for undertaking the foregoing discussion of the rationale for the consequentialist conception of the right was to put us in a position to assess the suggestion that once this rationale was exhibited, it might become evident that there is an equally satisfactory rationale available for agent-centred restrictions after all. Thus it is to an assessment of that suggestion that I now turn.

It seems to me that no plausible underlying motivation for the restrictions emerges from a consideration of the rationale for the consequentialist conception of the right. Indeed, fully agent-centred conceptions join with hybrid conceptions in rejecting the consequentialist procedure of allowing the principles of human conduct to be completely determined by an antecedently fixed conception of what the best overall sets of happenings would be. Both agree that an adequate conception of the right must embody a set of demands that it is reasonable to impose on the conduct of human agents, and that there are features of human agents in virtue of which it is rational to require of them something other than the constant production of the best states of affairs. If agent-centred restrictions are to be adequately motivated, what needs to be shown is that there is indeed some particular feature of human beings in virtue of which it is rational to prohibit them from doing what would lead to the best outcome overall. And a consideration of the rationale for the *consequentialist* conception of the right is clearly of no help in this regard.

There is, however, one final way in which a defender of agent-centred restrictions might try to show that this demand for a rationale for the restrictions is inappropriate. The argument might run as follows. If it is said that the restrictions require a rationale because there is something paradoxical about the idea that it is impermissible to commit one act of an objectionable type in order to minimize acts of the very same type, or other comparably objectionable events, the only 'rationale' the defender of the restrictions can, in fairness, be expected to offer, is that such acts are forbidden because they are wrong. No further rationale is possible or necessary. For, unlike consequentialist views, fully agent-centred conceptions do not regard the rightness or wrongness of an action as determined by its tendency to advance or defeat the overall good. Such conceptions embody a conviction that acts of certain types are wrong in and of themselves, and not because they are deficient in the promotion of some other kind of moral quantity. Consequentialists, the argument might continue, regard some things as *good* in and of themselves and other things as *bad* in and of themselves. And it is no more appropriate to demand some underlying principled rationale for fully agent-centred principles of right and wrong than it would be to demand such a rationale for a consequentialist conception of the good.

This argument seems to me unpersuasive. In the first place, although fully agent-centred conceptions do not regard the rightness or wrongness of an action as completely or exclusively determined by its tendency to advance or defeat the overall good, they do typically regard such tendencies as among the factors that can make an act right or wrong. As Rawls has said: 'All ethical doctrines worth our attention take consequences into account in judging rightness. One which did not would be simply irrational, crazy.'[4] Since fully agent-centred conceptions do not hold judgements about the rightness and wrongness of actions to be completely insensitive to considerations about the goodness and badness of their consequences, it is fair to ask why then, in circumstances where it is apparently irrational to forbid conduct that is guided by the consequences, that is precisely what such conceptions do.

Moreover, it does not constitute an adequate answer to this question to claim that agent-centred restrictions forbid doing certain things because it is wrong to do those things. It is entirely appropriate to demand some underlying rationale for the restrictions, just as it would indeed be legitimate to seek a rationale for a consequentialist conception of the good. Remember that some versions of consequentialism incorporate distribution-sensitive conceptions of the overall good, and that, in Chapter Three, a rationale for a certain kind of distribution-sensitive conception was in fact identified. And while no attempt was made to identify a rationale for the pluralistic conception of the *individual* good relied on by that type of distribution-sensitive ranking principle, it was in no way suggested that such an inquiry would be inappropriate. Remember too that hybrid conceptions, by virtue of incorporating an agent-centred prerogative, have non-consequentialist principles of right action, just as fully agent-centred conceptions do. Like fully agent-centred conceptions, hybrid views do not regard the rightness or wrongness of actions as completely determined by their tendency to promote or undermine the overall good. Yet it did of course prove possible to identify an underlying principled rationale for the prerogative. And there is every reason to search for a comparable rationale for agent-centred restrictions. For unless something can be said about *why* certain things and not others are regarded as wrong, such restrictions will inevitably tend to appear arbitrary and unmotivated, especially in view of their paradoxical air.

Thus, if my account in this chapter has been accurate, the demand for a rationale for agent-centred restrictions is not

[4] *A Theory of Justice*, p. 30.

inappropriate. A careful reconsideration of the structure of the investigation undertaken in this book has failed to reveal any hidden bias against the restrictions, or any other reason for setting aside the results arrived at in the course of that investigation. I therefore conclude this chapter as I did the last: by acknowledging that an adequate rationale for agent-centred restrictions still eludes us, by insisting that the elusiveness of that rationale is deeply troubling, and by expressing the hope that the genuine intuitive appeal of such restrictions will not blind us to the need to understand and explain them better, if we are to reaffirm their place in our moral universe with confidence.

INDEX